Advisory Committee on the Microbiological Safety of Food

Report on Salmonella in Eggs

*Advises the Government
on the Microbiological Safety of Food*

London:HMSO

CONTENTS

CHAPTER 6
USE AND HANDLING OF EGGS

CHAPTER 7
CONCLUSIONS

CHAPTER 8
RECOMMENDATIONS

APPENDICES

REFERENCES

BIBLIOGRAPHY

SUMMARY

1.   From the information presented to us, in the form of published scientific papers and written and oral evidence provided by a variety of individuals and organisations, the Working Group has attempted to assess the contribution made by eggs to human foodborne salmonellosis.

2.   *Salmonella enteritidis* phage type 4 is currently the most prevalent type of salmonella causing human infection in the UK. It has been shown that eggs can be infected with *Salmonella enteritidis* internally or externally by the time they are laid, or can subsequently become contaminated after lay. However, the relationship between the consumption of hens' eggs and human foodborne salmonella infection is far from simple.

3.   In only a relatively few foodborne outbreaks have investigations provided microbiological or statistical evidence from which to identify the vehicle of infection, and only small scale studies have been undertaken on vehicles of infection in sporadic cases. Analysis of the small number of outbreaks where sound evidence has made identification of the food vehicle possible has shown an association with eggs or foods containing them. However as eggs provide a good medium for bacterial growth, it is often difficult to determine the contribution made by eggs, as opposed to cross contamination due to poor kitchen hygiene or handling, when attempting to determine the cause of outbreaks of foodborne disease. We have therefore made recommendations for improving the investigation and reporting of foodborne disease outbreaks, and have also recommended that further studies be undertaken to ascertain the relative importance of the various factors that may contribute to their occurrence.

4.   After reviewing the data available, we consider that only a small percentage of eggs are contaminated with *Salmonella enteritidis*. However as millions of eggs are sold everyday the number contaminated will not be insubstantial. Nevertheless any risk posed to the individual from eggs contaminated with salmonella will be reduced if the eggs are not consumed raw or inadequately cooked.

5.   Taking all these elements into account, we believe that while eggs are undoubtedly an important source of human salmonella infection, the contribution that they make to the current levels of human salmonellosis cannot be quantified precisely. We have, however, made a number of recommendations to improve the way eggs are handled and stored, which should help to reduce any risk of human salmonella infection from eggs. In summary, the principal recommendations are :-

   i) we endorse the advice issued by the Chief Medical Officer that no-one should eat raw eggs, and that vulnerable groups, such as the elderly, the sick, babies and pregnant women, should eat only eggs that have been cooked until both the white and yolk are solid;

   ii) eggs should be used within 3 weeks of lay and "use-by" dates should be provided on egg packs, and possibly the eggs themselves;

   iii) eggs should be kept as at a constant temperature as far as possible during storage, transport and retailing and should never exceed an ambient temperature of 20°C; once purchased eggs should be stored in a refrigerator; and

   iv) pasteurised egg should be substituted for shell egg in dishes that are eaten raw or are only lightly cooked.

6.   Finally, we have reviewed the Government's measures for the control of salmonella in eggs and poultry and have noted that since the measures were introduced there has been a decline in the number of large laying flocks in which infection with *Salmonella enteritidis* has been confirmed. We therefore believe that the continuing need for the compulsory slaughter of infected laying flocks could now be reviewed.

TERMS OF REFERENCE

The Parliamentary Under Secretary of State for Health announced in the House of Commons on 12 June 1990 the establishment of the Advisory Committee on the Microbiological Safety of Food. The Committee was given the following terms of reference:-

"To assess the risk to humans of micro-organisms which are used or occur in or on food and to advise Ministers on the exercise of powers in the Food Safety Act 1990 relating to the microbiological safety of food".

LIST OF MEMBERS

CHAIRMAN

Professor Heather M. Dick MD, FIBiol, FRCP, S(Glas), FRCPath, FRSE
Professor of Medical Microbiology University of Dundee

MEMBERS

Dr. R. Gilbert	- Director, Food Hygiene Laboratory, Public Health Laboratory Service
Dr. T. Wilson	- Senior Consultant Bacteriologist, Belfast City Hospital Laboratory
Dr. N. A. Simmons	- Consultant Microbiologist, Department of Clinical Bacteriology, Guy's Hospital
Dr. S. Palmer	- Consultant Epidemiologist, Communicable Disease Surveillance Centre, Welsh Unit, Cardiff
Professor R. Feldman	- Professor of Clinical Epidemiology, London Hospital
Professor D. Georgala	- Director, Agriculture and Food Research Council, Institute of Food Research
Dr. .P .A Mullen	- Veterinary Advisor to Union International Ltd
Mr R. Southgate	- Technical Director, Northern Foods Meat Group
Mr G. Amery OBE	- Group General Manager, Technical Group, CWS Ltd
Dr. G. Spriegel	- Director of Scientific Services, Sainsbury's
Mr R. Ackerman	- Chairman of Hotel and Catering Training Company
Dr. M. Stringer	- Director of Food Science Division, Campden Food and Drink Research Association
Mr R. Sprenger	- Director of Environmental Services, Doncaster
Dr. C. St. J. Buxton	- Director of Public Health, Durham Health Authority
Dame Rachel Waterhouse OBE	- Past Chairman, Consumers' Association
Mrs B. Saunders	- Freelance Consultant, for Consumer Affairs

ASSESSORS

Mr K. Baker	- MAFF (To July 1991)
Dr. R. Cawthorne	- MAFF (From July 1991)
Mr R. Alexander	- Welsh Office
Mr E. Davison	- Scottish Office Agriculture and Fisheries Department
Dr. H. Denner	- MAFF
Mr B. Dickinson	- MAFF
Dr. C. McMurray	- Department of Agriculture Northern Ireland
Dr. E. Mitchell	- Department of Health and Social Security (Northern Ireland)
Ms D. Pease	- Department of Health
Dr. N. Peel	- Public Health Laboratory Service
Dr. R. Skinner	- Scottish Office (HHD) (to September 1991)
Dr. A. McLeod	- Scottish Office (HHD) (from September 1991)

SECRETARIAT

Mrs S. Gordon Brown	- Department of Health
Dr. D. Harper	- Department of Health
Dr. C. Swinson	- Department of Health
Dr. R. Mitchell	- MAFF
Dr. D. Lees	- MAFF

WORKING GROUP ON SALMONELLA IN EGGS

LIST OF MEMBERS

CHAIRMAN
Professor Heather M. Dick

MEMBERS
Dr. R. Gilbert
Mr R. Southgate
Dr. M. Stringer
Mr R. Sprenger
Dr. S. Palmer

ASSESSORS
Dr. R. Cawthorne   - Ministry of Agriculture Fisheries and Food
Ms L. Lockyer   - Department of Health (to July 1991)
Mr T. Murray   - Department of Health (from July 1991 to June 1992)
Mr C. Lister   - Department of Health (from June 1992)

SECRETARIAT
Dr. L. Robinson   - Department of Health
Dr. D. Harper   - Department of Health
Dr. D. Lees   - MAFF (from January 1992)

CHAPTER 1

INTRODUCTION

1.1   Although members of the genus Salmonella have long been recognised as an important cause of human food poisoning, the emergence of *Salmonella enteritidis* as the most common serotype isolated from humans in Great Britain has been a relatively recent phenomenon.

1.2   In August 1988, following concerns that eggs could be a possible source of salmonellosis in humans, the Chief Medical Officer advised consumers to avoid eating raw eggs or uncooked foods[1] made from them, and in December 1988 also advised that vulnerable people such as the elderly, the sick, babies and pregnant women should consume only eggs which had been cooked until the white and yolk were solid[2]. This advice still stands.

1.3   The relevance of salmonella in eggs in relation to human health was covered in detail and reported on by the House of Commons Select Committee on Agriculture, in reports presented to Parliament in February 1989[3] and December 1989[4]. In January 1991, the Committee on the Microbiological Safety of Food (Chairman: Sir Mark Richmond), noted that the Government had introduced a wide- ranging package of controls on salmonella in eggs and poultry[a], but considered that it was too early to judge the effectiveness of these measures[5], and recommended that the new Advisory Committee on the Microbiological Safety of Food return to the subject of salmonella in eggs early in its deliberations.

1.4   In March 1991, the Advisory Committee agreed that it should carry out a further investigation of the relationship between eggs and salmonella infections in humans. We were asked by the Committee to examine the existing evidence and to identify what further experimental evidence might be needed to clarify the issue. The Committee agreed that the Working Group's terms of reference would be:-

"to consider to what extent eggs are responsible for the incidence of foodborne disease due to salmonella, and to propose advice for the Advisory Committee to convey to Ministers."

BACKGROUND AND SCOPE OF THE REVIEW

1.5   The Working Group was concerned to ensure that its examination would take into account relevant scientific information. Organisations and established experts were therefore invited to provide references to published papers and to submit additional factual information which they considered relevant to the Group's terms of reference. A list of respondents is at Appendix I. We also asked the organisations and experts listed at Appendix II to give oral evidence, the main points of which are summarised at Appendix III. We wish to place on record our appreciation to all those concerned for their co-operation and assistance.

1.6   During the course of the review, we sought to establish whether sound scientific information was available on the following points:

i)   any factors which may have contributed to the increased incidence of *Salmonella enteritidis* in poultry and humans in Great Britain;

ii)   the incidence of *Salmonella enteritidis* in Great Britain as compared with that in other countries in Europe and the USA;

iii)   the possible reasons for the lower reported incidence in Northern Ireland;

---

a   poultry is defined as domestic fowl in the context of this report.

iv)   the possible reason(s) for the emergence of *Salmonella enteritidis* phage type 4 as the predominant phage type in Europe;

v)   the incidence, epidemiology and spread of infection in the national poultry flock including whether and, by what route contamination may be introduced into a flock previously recorded as infection free;

vi)   the ways in which eggs become contaminated;

vii)   the extent of contamination of imported shell eggs and the proportion of eggs sold in the UK which are imported;

viii)   the extent of contamination of shell eggs produced and sold in the UK;

ix)   the extent to which storage and temperature regimes from point of lay to the point of sale affect the level of contamination of eggs; and

x)   the extent to which changes in catering practices in the last few years may have contributed to the risk of human infection.

CHAPTER 2

EPIDEMIOLOGY OF HUMAN SALMONELLOSIS

Sources and Vehicles of Infection

2.1   Salmonellae are Gram-negative, motile, rod-shaped bacteria that can grow in both aerobic and anaerobic conditions, at temperatures between 7°C and 48°C, at pH 4 to 8 and at water activities above 0.93[6]. They are resistant to freezing and drying. The organisms are ubiquitous and can be isolated from the gut contents of animals including wild birds, domestic pets, and rodents. Certain types of salmonellae may be associated with particular animal species. Salmonellae have also been isolated from food, milk and animal products, and foodborne illness may occur after consuming food or drink contaminated with these organisms. Infection may also be acquired from an infected person by the faecal-oral route when the standard of hygiene is poor.

The Nature of the Illness

2.2   The spectrum of illness caused by salmonellae may range from a mild gastro-intestinal upset which may not warrant seeking medical advice, to a more severe debilitating illness which may require admission to hospital. In some instances these organisms may cause septicaemia or death (68 people died from salmonella related disease in England and Wales in 1990). Gastro-intestinal symptoms generally occur between 12 and 36 hours after consuming contaminated food or drink but may take as long as 72 hours or longer to appear. Diarrhoea, nausea, abdominal pain, vomiting, headache and fever are the predominant symptoms, lasting for at least 24-72 hours and often longer. Where vomiting and diarrhoea are particularly severe, resulting in dehydration, the patient may require hospital treatment. Short term excretion occurs, but long term excretion is rare.

Salmonella Surveillance

England and Wales

2.3   In England and Wales the Public Health Laboratory Service (PHLS) Laboratory for Enteric Pathogens (LEP) (formerly the Division of Enteric Pathogens (DEP)) receives salmonella isolates for precise identification and confirmation from human infections from PHLS and National Health Service (NHS) laboratories. Collation of this data has allowed trends in incidence to be identified. Isolates from animals and poultry are also received from MAFF Veterinary laboratories, and on occasions isolates from food and other sources are received from a variety of other laboratories.

2.4   Until the end of 1991, the PHLS Communicable Disease Surveillance Centre (CDSC) provided an additional salmonella surveillance system whereby PHLS and NHS laboratories voluntarily reported to them salmonella isolates from human infections. From 1 January 1992 the DEP and CDSC databases were amalgamated into one PHLS salmonella surveillance system, in accordance with a recommendation from the Committee on the Microbiological Safety of Food[7] and following the development of a new computer system. The data is now patient-based rather than based on individual isolations. Duplication of data when people are tested more than once is therefore avoided. Details of the infection are sent on a single report form to LEP and may be accompanied by a clinical specimen. This information is automatically relayed to the CDSC.

2.5   CDSC receives voluntary information on outbreaks[b] of foodborne illness from medical

---

b   the CDSC definition of an outbreak is an incident in which two or more people are thought to have had a common exposure, experienced a similar illness, or a proven infection.

personnel and Environmental Health Officers (EHOs). These reports are made on standard forms which are cross-checked to identify any duplication. CDSC does not receive formal information on all outbreaks, but it may receive informal information from a range of sources, for example from medical practitioners, and from reports in the local and national press. We believe this situation should be improved, through further development of outbreak reoprting arrangements.

2.6   Statistics on Salmonella infection appear in the Communicable Disease Report published by the PHLS. Data on salmonella incidents in animals and birds[c] reported under the Zoonoses Order 1989[8] are published annually by Agriculture Departments in 'Animal Salmonellosis'. In addition, the PHLS and the State Veterinary Service (SVS) publish quarterly the Update on Salmonella Infection which gives both human and animal data on salmonella infection.

Scotland

2.7   Since 1989 salmonella infection has been included in the list of reportable infections, details of which are sent weekly by all microbiology laboratories to the Communicable Diseases (Scotland) Unit (CD(S)U). Isolates are sent to the Scottish Salmonella Reference Library at Stobhill Hospital, Glasgow for precise identification.

2.8   Outbreaks are investigated by Consultants in Public Health Medicine and Environmental Health Officers in individual Health Board and Local Authority Areas. Reports are sent to CD(S)U on standard forms.

2.9   Data on the levels of infection in Scotland, which include details of all isolates from NHS laboratories and from the Veterinary Investigation Laboratories in the Scottish Agriculture College and the Veterinary Schools, are published in the Weekly Report of the Communicable Diseases (Scotland) Unit and are summarised in the annual report "Salmonellosis - Summary of Isolates in Scotland" also produced by CD(S)U.

Northern Ireland

2.10   In Northern Ireland laboratory-confirmed infections which may be of food origin are reported by the 18 hospital laboratories in the Province to the Department of Health and Social Services Northern Ireland (DHSS(NI)), and are also copied to CDSC.

2.11   There is no systematic reporting of outbreaks to DHSS (NI) at present although large outbreaks would be reported centrally in order to facilitate the coordination of investigation. A reporting system comparable to that of CDSC is expected to be introduced in the Province in the near future.

2.12   Data on the incidence of infection are published in the Monthly Report Communicable Diseases Northern Ireland. Cumulative annual data are provided in the last issue of the year.

Epidemiology of salmonella infection in the UK

2.13   There are over 2,200 serological types of salmonella that can cause gastro-intestinal illness, but in any one year only about 200 types are usually confirmed at DEP.

2.14   In England and Wales salmonella isolations reported from human infections doubled from 10,251 in 1981 to 20,532 in 1987. The number in 1991 was 27,693 (see Appendix IV). These figures may, in reality, underestimate the actual number of persons affected, as many with symptoms

---

c   an incident is defined as the reported isolation of salmonella from an animal or bird, a group of animals or birds, or from animal or bird products or surroundings which can be related to identifiable animals. If more than one species is infected from a common source separate incidents are reported from each species.

will not seek medical help. If they do, faecal samples will only be sent to laboratories in a proportion of cases. Others may be asymptomatic, and therefore unaware that they have the infection. The Human Epidemiology Working Group of the Steering Group on the Microbiological Safety of Food has set up pilot studies to assess the feasibility of national studies to estimate the true incidence of infectious intestinal disease in the population and to give more information on the nature of the infecting organisms and routes of infection.

2.15 In Northern Ireland the rate of human isolations has always been lower than for the rest of the UK (see Appendix IV).

2.16 At present, the three most common serotypes isolated from humans in the UK are *Salmonella enteritidis*, *Salmonella typhimurium* and *Salmonella virchow*. In 1991 they formed 63%, 19% and 3% respectively of the human salmonella isolations in England and Wales reported to DEP. Although particular serotypes may remain prevalent for a number of years, it is likely that, as in the past, other serotypes will come to the fore. There is no clear explanation for this well observed phenomenon but it is likely to be related to the prevalence of these organisms in food at the time.

Epidemiology of Salmonella Infection in Europe and the USA

2.17 Problems with *Salmonella enteritidis* infection are not confined to the UK; similar situations have arisen in Europe, the USA and other areas of the world[9]. The recently published Fifth Report of the World Health Organisation (WHO) Surveillance Programme for Foodborne Infections and Intoxications in Europe for 1985-1989 shows that for the majority of European countries, salmonellae are the cause of most foodborne infections. *Salmonella enteritidis* is the commonest reported salmonella serotype isolated not only in the UK but also in Austria, Bulgaria, Czechoslovakia, Finland, France, Germany, Hungary, Norway, Poland, Romania, Spain and Switzerland[10].

2.18 In the north-eastern United States of America there was a greater than six-fold rise in human infection due to *Salmonella enteritidis* between 1976 and 1986[11]. Between January 1985 and May 1987 there were 65 foodborne outbreaks due to this organism, and in 35 of those where a food vehicle was identified, 27 were caused by Grade A[d] shell eggs or foods that contained these eggs. American national data from 1973 to 1984 showed that *Salmonella enteritidis* outbreaks were more frequently linked to egg-containing foods than outbreaks of other salmonella serotypes.

2.19 Similarly, there was a five-fold increase in the number of outbreaks caused by *Salmonella enteritidis* in Spain between 1977 and 1984[12]. Home-made mayonnaise is considered to have been an important vehicle of infection[13]. Data from the Basque region suggested that *Salmonella enteritidis* was responsible for 78% of outbreaks of known aetiology, and eggs and foods containing egg were believed to be the vehicle in 90% of salmonella outbreaks[14].

2.20 In Italy it was reported that from 1982 to 1988 there was a five-fold increase in human isolations of *Salmonella enteritidis*. Isolations of salmonella from non-human sources are not often reported in Italy, but between 1978 and 1988 *Salmonella enteritidis* was isolated from 88 food samples of which 42 (48%) were from eggs or poultry[15].

2.21 According to a WHO report, there was a large outbreak of *Salmonella enteritidis* infection in the German Democratic Republic in 1987, which involved 1,623 people[16]. The outbreak was associated with consumption of a food containing raw eggs, and the same *Salmonella enteritidis* phage type was isolated from the poultry farm where the eggs were produced in the same year.

---

d   Grade A shell eggs are fresh, clean undamaged eggs which must meet official stringent requirements in relation to their contents. The characteristics of eggs classified as Grade A in the UK are at Appendix VII. In the USA Grade A eggs may be washed but washing is not permitted in the UK.

Connections between Illness and Food

2.22   From the Spring of 1988 onwards there was a marked increase in reports to CDSC of outbreaks of foodborne infection due to *Salmonella enteritidis* which were attributed to eggs or food containing eggs, for example, mayonnaise. Between 1989 and 1991 CDSC received reports of 2,767[e] outbreaks in England and Wales of which 2,375 were family outbreaks and 392 were general outbreaks (Table 1). About half of both family and general outbreaks were due to *Salmonella enteritidis* phage type 4.

2.23   Analysis of the reports of general outbreaks, performed in a manner similar to that done for the House of Commons Select Committee on Agriculture in 1989, showed that a food vehicle was identified in a total of 56% of the 392 outbreaks. In 22% of the outbreaks the food vehicle was identified by microbiological or statistical means, and 45% of these food vehicles contained eggs[17]. In no case was the food containing egg made from pasteurised egg.

2.24   The investigation of foodborne illness to determine the vehicle and route of infection is often complex and time-consuming. We believe there is a need for clear guidance to help those involved with these investigations so that appropriate information is gathered in a consistent way. This should help to ensure that the conclusions reached have a sound basis and the data gathered are useful for national surveillance. We understand that the Department of Health have taken steps to develop such guidance and we welcome this initiative.

2.25   The relatively high proportion of outbreak reports to CDSC in which evidence to confirm food vehicles appears to be lacking has led some observers to express doubt about the representativeness of these data. To examine this a retrospective review of all general salmonella outbreaks in Wales between 1985 and 1990 was undertaken[18]. This showed that in 20 of 23 (87%) outbreaks a vehicle was confirmed by isolation of the organism from food, or by either case control or cohort studies or by means of both methods; 10 of 13 *Salmonella enteritidis* phage type 4 outbreaks were linked to foods containing eggs compared with only 2 of 10 other outbreaks. Despite the lack of direct evidence to identify the source in these general outbreaks the data provided strong indirect evidence that eggs were often the source of *Salmonella enteritidis* phage type 4 infection in these cases.

2.26   We understand that a similar review of general outbreaks is currently being conducted in England. In January 1992 CDSC introduced a new surveillance scheme for outbreaks of gastro-intestinal disease and will now routinely collect information on the evidence which led to the identification of the reported food vehicles. We welcome this initiative and believe that it will significantly assist the interpretation of outbreak data.

2.27   The epidemiological evidence to implicate whole shell hens' eggs as the vehicle or possible source of infection for sporadic[f] cases of *Salmonella enteritidis* phage type 4 is not so clear. Two case control studies have been reported in the United Kingdom. One carried out in Wales was a small study of 24 cases[19]. These cases were significantly more likely than well people in the same households to have eaten egg or foods containing eggs in the three days before onset of illness. No differences were found in the consumption of chicken. In the other larger case-control study of 232 cases in England[20], it was found that eating raw egg or shop bought sandwiches containing mayonnaise or egg were significant risk factors. Eating cooked egg was as common in controls as in cases, but if eggs were eaten cases were more likely to have eaten them lightly cooked. Consumption of pre-cooked hot chicken was also associated with illness. However, these foods together could only explain less than 40% of the cases. We believe that further studies are needed to investigate the sources and vehicles of infection of sporadic cases.

---

e   provisional data

f   sporadic cases are those that occur singly, that is unconnected with any others.

TABLE 2.1: OUTBREAKS OF *SALMONELLA ENTERITIDIS* IN ENGLAND AND WALES REPORTED TO CDSC 1989-1991

		1989	1990	1991
All outbreaks	Total	935	896	936
	Family	813	777	785
	General	122	119	151
Outbreaks with a vehicle reported (but not necessarily confirmed)				
	Total	113	103	139
	Family	44	39	52
	General	69	64	87
Outbreaks with vehicle containing egg				
	Total	42	52	57
	Family	19	22	25
	General	23	30	32
Outbreaks with other vehicles				
	Total	71	51	82
	Family	25	17	27
	General	46	34	55

Source: PHLS unpublished provisional data

2.28 To aid epidemiological investigations there is a need to differentiate further between sub-types of *Salmonella enteritidis* phage type 4, and we believe that there is a need for further research into the sub-typing of this organism.

Summary of Conclusions and Recommendations

2.29 From 1981 to 1991 there has been a rise of over 170% in the reported number of cases of salmonella in humans, primarily because of an increase in *Salmonella enteritidis* infections, particularly *Salmonella enteritidis* phage type 4.

2.30 Other countries in the world, notably in Europe and the USA, have seen similar rises in human salmonellosis which appear to have started at about the same time as that in the UK.

2.31 Northern Ireland has a lower rate of human salmonellosis than the rest of the UK. Human isolations there have steadily declined since 1987.

2.32 Most cases of salmonella infection occur sporadically. Salmonella outbreaks contribute only a small proportion of cases to the total number of reported illnesses. Salmonella surveillance data shows that the number of general outbreaks in the UK has not significantly increased in recent years despite the increase in cases.

2.33 Although it is not clear why *Salmonella enteritidis* has become the predominant serotype causing human infection in the UK, it is most probable that it is due to its presence in certain foods, in particular eggs and poultry.

2.34 Microbiological and epidemiological data from the UK and abroad have shown a strong association between *Salmonella enteritidis* and the consumption of eggs and poultry or foods containing them. Data from thoroughly investigated salmonella outbreaks while not always providing direct evidence to identify the source(s) of the infection, have provided strong indirect evidence that eggs have been the source in *Salmonella enteritidis* outbreaks. In many investigations the putative vehicle of infection is no longer available for testing and is not traceable back to the supplier. Therefore there is currently insufficient information available to enable us to assess what proportion of cases (both sporadic and in outbreaks) are due to the consumption of eggs and foods containing eggs.

CHAPTER 3

EPIDEMIOLOGY OF SALMONELLA IN POULTRY FLOCKS

Background

3.1   *Salmonella enteritidis* appears to be well adapted to poultry. Although it can cause mortality among young chicks, it rarely causes clinical disease in adult birds. It is now the most common salmonella serotype reported from poultry, representing 36%[21] of all incidents reported in 1991 under the Zoonoses Order 1989[8].

3.2   Although the majority of salmonellae are found in the intestines and are excreted in the faeces, some such as *Salmonella enteritidis* have been demonstrated to have the ability to invade the body and infect internal organs including ovarian tissue. The invasive ability of *Salmonella enteritidis* and thus the potential to contaminate egg contents before they are laid, has implications both for the transmission of infection to man and the vertical transmission of infection to birds in the breeding and production pyramid.

Levels of Infection

3.3   Incidents of *Salmonella enteritidis* in poultry reported under the Zoonoses Order 1975 were increasing at around the same time as the levels of incidence were rising in humans. There were only 15 incidents in 1985, rising to 36 in 1986, 111 in 1987 and 261 in 1988.

Sources and Vehicles of Infection

3.4   The rise in the incidence of *Salmonella enteritidis* in poultry which has taken place since 1985 is not unique to Great Britain, a similar rise having been observed in other EC Member States, North America and various other parts of the world. It is difficult to be precise about when or by what route the organism was introduced into poultry in Great Britain.

3.5   It has been suggested to us that the organism may have entered the poultry breeding population via feedingstuffs, possibly raw materials or additives, and because of its propensity to invade internal organs such as the ovary and oviduct, thereafter spread vertically to the production sector. The Expert Group on Animal Feedingstuffs (chaired by Professor E Lamming) have reviewed the data on salmonella contamination in feedingstuffs and raw materials available from a range of sources[22]. They noted that there were serious difficulties in trying to assess the contribution feed may make to the carriage of salmonella in animals and that the predominant serotype found in feedingstuffs and feed ingredients was not *Salmonella enteritidis*. They concluded that although there were examples from previous outbreaks of salmonella serotypes introduced via feedingstuffs causing animal and human infections, there is generally insufficiently robust data on salmonella contamination in feedingstuffs to allow a link to be established between previous feed contamination and the current infection/ contamination in animals. They also concluded that the removal of feed contamination alone at this stage would not necessarily have a significant effect on current *Salmonella enteritidis* in the human population.

3.6   It has also been suggested that genetic selection of the elite stock comprising the pinnacle of the breeding pyramids for both the egg and poultrymeat sectors may have brought about an increased susceptibility to infection. There are two main strains of layer breeding birds in the UK, and production of nucleus breeding stock is restricted to a few companies in the Netherlands and France, one strain from each country. There is no evidence to suggest that *Salmonella enteritidis* infection is now present in mainstream commercial grandparent/elite stock maintained in the United Kingdom or that the present genetic make-up of poultry stock has brought about a susceptibility to infection with *Salmonella enteritidis* phage type 4.

17

3.7   Present strains of *Salmonella enteritidis* may be more invasive although there is no convincing evidence that they are more virulent. Infection can be transmitted via the aerosol route which has implications for spread of infection in hatcheries and within buildings. Once introduced, infection may be spread via drinking water and feed contaminated from the environment. The Committee on the Microbiological Safety of Food recommended that the Government should produce guidelines on the hygienic design of broilerhouses, including their water supply and distribution systems[7]. We believe that similar guidelines would be of benefit to the egg production sector.

3.8   Difficulty may be experienced in eradicating infection from poultry houses unless considerable attention is paid to the cleansing and disinfection of equipment and the internal environment between crops of birds and the hygienic disposal of litter and faeces. This may be difficult to achieve in older houses and those with earth floors. Two Codes of Practice were produced in 1988 which were of help to the egg production sector - a MAFF/British Poultry Federation Code on the control of salmonellae in commercial laying flocks[23] and a Code of Practice for Poultry Health Scheme Members, which also covers hatcheries and breeding flocks[24]. The Codes are now 4 years old and we believe that they should be updated.

3.9   The administration of a mixture of harmless microorganisms from the intestines of healthy chickens to chicks has been shown to interfere with the ability of salmonella to colonise the gastro-intestinal tract. This principle, known as 'competitive exclusion', has been shown to be of use in reducing the incidence of infection with salmonellae in broiler flocks[25]. However, the longevity of laying flocks in comparison with broiler flocks may mean that it will be of less use to the egg industry, although more work needs to be done before any firm conclusions can be reached.

3.10   The maintenance of salmonellae in the environment is by complex pathways, and rodents and wild birds may act as important reservoirs of infection. The current role of rodents in the transmission or maintenance of salmonellas on farms is uncertain. Nevertheless we believe that effective controls are essential. In addition, the possibility of infection being transmitted on the clothes and footware of personnel should not be overlooked, and poultry workers should adopt specific measures to prevent cross-contamination from poultry workers to poultry flocks and vice-versa.

3.11   The levels of *Salmonella enteritidis* in poultry stocks in Northern Ireland appear to be lower than those in the rest of the UK. It should be recognised that in the Province there is a much smaller poultry industry which has actively participated with producers and authorities in safeguarding the health of their stock. It has been suggested to us that this control of *Salmonella enteritidis* in poultry may have contributed to the lower levels of human infection in the Province.

Introduction of Control Measures

3.12   In response to the increased number of outbreaks of human salmonellosis associated with eggs, the Government introduced a comprehensive programme of measures for the control of salmonella in eggs and poultry in 1989. The measures had two important aims. First, to protect public health by identifying and removing laying flocks infected with *Salmonella enteritidis* or *Salmonella typhimurium*; second, the long term reduction of infection throughout the production chain from the supply of feedingstuffs to the production of healthy breeding stock.

3.13   Legislative powers were introduced which (a) placed an obligation on owners of poultry flocks and processors or importers of processed animal protein to undertake regular bacteriological monitoring of birds or product on their premises or in their possession and (b) required all isolations of salmonella to be notified to the Ministry of Agriculture, Fisheries and Food. These statutory requirements were supplemented by the introduction and adoption of voluntary Codes of Practice for the control of salmonella in feedingstuffs[26,27], laying flocks[23], breeding flocks[24] and broilers[28] and were backed up by a programme of research. Since its introduction in March 1989, the programme has been kept under careful review and changes have been made in the light of developing knowledge and expertise.

Legislation

3.14 Under the Zoonoses Order 1989[8], all isolations of salmonella from samples taken from an animal or bird, or from the carcase, products or surroundings of an animal or bird or from any feeding stuff, must be reported to a Veterinary Officer of the Ministry of Agriculture, Fisheries and Food. In practice, reports are made to the Veterinary Investigation Officer in charge of one of the Ministry's Veterinary Investigation Centres in England and Wales or to the Divisional Veterinary Officer in Scotland. The Order also allows Veterinary Inspectors to enter any premises and carry out such enquiries as are considered necessary to determine whether salmonella is present. Powers are also available to declare a premises infected, to prohibit the movement of animals, poultry, carcases, products and feedingstuffs in or out of the premises except under licence, and to serve notices requiring the cleansing and disinfection of premises where salmonella is known to have been present. The Order also applies certain provisions of the Animal Health Act 1981[29] to organisms of the genus Salmonella, including powers relating to the compulsory slaughter of poultry.

3.15 The Poultry Laying Flocks (Testing and Registration etc) Order 1989[30], requires owners of flocks comprising 100 or more laying hens to register with the Ministry of Agriculture, Fisheries and Food (MAFF). In addition, owners of flocks comprising not less than 25 birds which are kept for the production of eggs for human consumption (including birds being reared for this purpose), or flocks comprising less than 25 birds the eggs from which are sold for human consumption, must take cloacal swabs or composite faeces samples from each house of birds comprising the flock and have them tested for salmonella in a MAFF authorised laboratory in accordance with the schedule laid down in the Order. Birds being reared must be tested when they are 3-5 weeks and 14 weeks of age, while adult birds must be tested every 12 weeks while in lay.

3.16 The Poultry Breeding Flocks and Hatcheries (Registration and Testing) Order 1989[31] requires the owners of all breeding flocks comprising 25 or more birds, and hatcheries with an incubator capacity of 1000 eggs or more, to register with MAFF. Owners of breeding flocks and hatcheries must also take samples from birds or their progeny and have them tested for salmonella in a MAFF authorised laboratory in accordance with the schedules laid down in the Order. In the case of birds being reared, chick box liners, cloacal swabs or composite faeces samples must be taken from day old chicks and birds aged 3-5 and 14 weeks of age. The progeny of adult birds are monitored through the hatchery, samples of chick meconium, chicks dead in shell or live chicks from each breeding premises supplying a hatchery being taken each week while the adult birds are in lay. Samples are taken every fourth week under MAFF supervision and are examined in a MAFF Veterinary Investigation Centre.

Operation of the Programme in Respect of Laying and Layer Breeder Flocks

3.17 When *Salmonella enteritidis* is isolated from a laying flock and is reported to MAFF under the Zoonoses Order 1989[8], a notice is served on the premises declaring it to be an infected place and prohibiting the movement of eggs and birds onto or off the premises except under licence. An investigation is then carried out by the Ministry's Veterinary Investigation Service in which a statistical sample of up to 59 birds is taken from each house on the premises and subjected to a detailed bacteriological examination. The sample size depends on the number of birds in the house, and is that required to give 95% probability of including at least one positive bird if the prevalence of infection in the flock is five per cent or more.

3.18 If *Salmonella enteritidis* is isolated from the sample of birds taken from a house, all the birds in that house are compulsorily slaughtered and the owner compensated. Prior to 26 March 1990 birds were slaughtered on farm and their carcases disposed of by burial or incineration. From that date, however, new arrangements for slaughter and heat processing of carcases were introduced such that birds can be slaughtered at an approved slaughterhouse and the carcases heat treated. Tests are carried out to ensure that heat treatment is effective. Veterinary and technical staff supervise the slaughter and heat processing at all stages and particular attention is paid to ensuring that the welfare of the birds is protected at all times. If slaughterhouse capacity is not available, or the numbers of birds are too small to make the operation economic, birds may still be slaughtered on farm. Owners of flocks in which *Salmonella enteritidis* infection has been confirmed also have the option of sending eggs from the flock for pasteurisation but in practice there is no demand for such material.

3.19 Once the birds have been removed, a notice is served under the Zoonoses Order 1989[8] requiring the house to be cleansed and disinfected. The house may not be restocked until it has been inspected by the Ministry and until environmental samples taken from the house and its equipment by MAFF staff have been shown to be free of salmonella.

3.20 These arrangements also apply when an isolation of either *Salmonella enteritidis* or *Salmonella typhimurium* is reported from a layer breeder flock. Investigations are also carried out when eggs are thought to be the source of infection in human food poisoning incidents caused by *Salmonella enteritidis* and the flock producing the eggs can be identified.

Results of the Government's Measures to Date

Laying flocks

3.21 Since the Government's measures were introduced in 1989, *Salmonella enteritidis* has been confirmed in 201 pullet and layer flocks and 1,755,862 birds have been compulsorily slaughtered (Table 1). There has been a decline in the number of birds compulsorily slaughtered; 179,828 layers and 68,445 pullets in 1991 compared with 437,967 layers and 205,861 pullets in 1989 (Table 1).

3.22 *Salmonella enteritidis* was confirmed in 58 laying flocks in 1989, 46 in 1990 and 61 in 1991. 38 of the 53 laying flocks (66%) and four of the eight pullet flocks compulsorily slaughtered in 1991 comprised less than 1,000 birds compared with 35.5% of the laying flocks and 0% of the pullet flocks slaughtered in 1989 (Table 2 and Table 3) indicating that *Salmonella enteritidis* infection is being confirmed in fewer large flocks. The estimated prevalence of *Salmonella enteritidis* infection in the 53 laying flocks compulsorily slaughtered in 1991 averaged 10.03% (range 1.8% - 33.1%), while for the 8 pullet flocks slaughtered the average was 18.5% (range 3.6% - 44.5%).

3.23 When the Government's measures were introduced in 1989, the controls adopted applied, as now, to isolations of *Salmonella enteritidis* from commercial laying flocks, but also applied to isolations of *Salmonella typhimurium*. In January 1991, the arrangements for dealing with *Salmonella enteritidis* from laying flocks were modified after it had become apparent that outbreaks of human *Salmonella typhimurium* food poisoning had fallen significantly in the previous year, and the number of outbreaks of *Salmonella typhimurium* food poisoning linked with eggs was extremely low. On 14 January 1991, the automatic slaughter policy for laying flocks infected with *Salmonella typhimurium* was discontinued although the arrangements for monitoring and reporting such isolates continues.

Layer breeders

3.24 *Salmonella enteritidis* has been confirmed in a total of 12 layer breeder flocks since 1989 and a total of 49,710 birds have been compulsorily slaughtered. However, three of these flocks comprising 13,016 birds were outside the mainstream commercial breeding flocks and 4 flocks comprising 18,118 birds represented a continuing episode in the same flock.

EC Zoonoses Proposal

3.25 On September 12 1991, the EC Commission published a proposal for a Council Regulation for the control of salmonella and specified zoonoses in animals and products of animal origin in all Member States of the European Community. The proposal is currently being discussed by a Council Working Group. It contains provisions for the monitoring and control of *Salmonella enteritidis* and *Salmonella typhimurium* in commercial breeding flocks, laying flocks and hatcheries.

TABLE 3.1: THE TOTAL NUMBER OF LAYER AND LAYER BREEDER FLOCKS INFECTED WITH *SALMONELLA ENTERITIDIS* AND COMPULSORILY SLAUGHTERED IN GREAT BRITAIN

Type of bird	Flocks[1]				Birds slaughtered[2]			
	1989	1990	1991	1992	1989	1990	1991	1992
Layers	58	46	61	36	643,822	581,682	248,273	282,085
- caged	22	27	26	17	237,758	476,160	169,669	183,255
- free range	23	11	27	14	200,203	4,275	10,159	25,253
- pullet	13	8	8	5	205,861	101,247	68,445	73,577
Layer breeders	0	3	7	2	0	5,936	35,756	8,018
Total	**58**	**49**	**68**	**38**	**643,822**	**587,618**	**284,029**	**290,103**

[1] - Based on 1991 Agricultural Census data
[2] - As of 3 July 1992
Source: MAFF unpublished data

TABLE 3.2: THE NUMBER OF ADULT LAYING FLOCKS IN WHICH *SALMONELLA ENTERITIDIS* HAS BEEN CONFIRMED COMPARED WITH THE TOTAL NUMBER AND SIZE OF FLOCKS IN GREAT BRITAIN

National (GB) figures			No. holdings on which Se confirmed			
Flock Size	No. holdings	No.birds	1989	1990	1991	1992[2]
1-24	24,387	268,695	0	2	5	2
25-999	5,315	597,290	16	20	33	18
1000-4999	802	2,024,100	7	4	7	5
5000-20,000	516	5,402,326	14	4	4	5
20,000+	260	22,009,804	8	8	4	1
Total	**31,280**	**30,302,215**	**45**	**38**	**53**	**31**

[1]-Based on 1991 Agricultural Census data
[2]-As of 3 July 1992
Source: MAFF unpublished data

TABLE 3.3: THE NUMBER AND SIZE OF PULLET REARING FLOCKS IN WHICH *SALMONELLA ENTERITIDIS* HAS BEEN CONFIRMED COMPARED WITH THE TOTAL NUMBER AND SIZE OF FLOCKS IN GREAT BRITAIN

National(GB) figures[1]			No. holdings on which which Se confirmed			
Flock Size	No. holdings	No.birds	1989	1990	1991	1992[2]
1-24	2,349	20,776	0	0	2	0
25-999	685	116,423	0	0	2	1
1000-4999	165	391,159	2	0	1	0
5000-20,000	184	1,845,226	5	6	0	3
20,000+	125	7,668,665	6	2	3	1
Total	**3,508**	**10,042,249**	**13**	**8**	**8**	**5**

[1] - Based on 1991 Agricultural Census data
[2] - As of 3 July 1992
Source: MAFF unpublished data EC Zoonoses proposal

Poultry Flocks slaughtered 1989-1992 because of <u>Salmonella enteritidis</u>

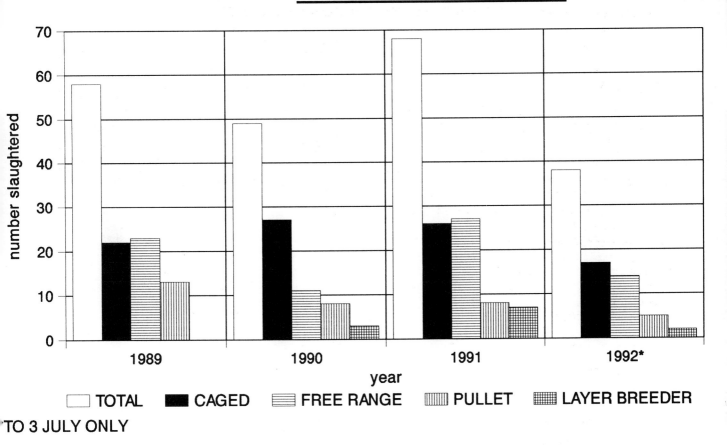

TOTAL ☐   CAGED ■   FREE RANGE ☰   PULLET ⫿   LAYER BREEDER ▦

*TO 3 JULY ONLY

Poultry (birds) slaughtered 1989-1992 because of <u>Salmonella enteritidis</u>

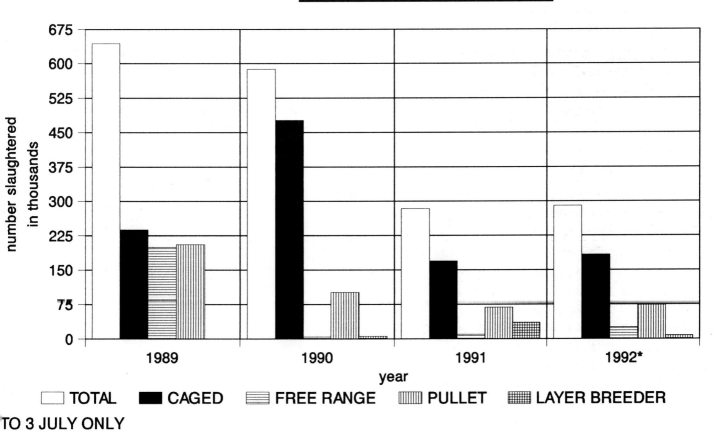

TOTAL ☐   CAGED ■   FREE RANGE ☰   PULLET ⫿   LAYER BREEDER ▦

*TO 3 JULY ONLY

NUMBER OF PULLET FLOCKS AND BIRDS BY FLOCK SIZE: ENGLAND AND WALES

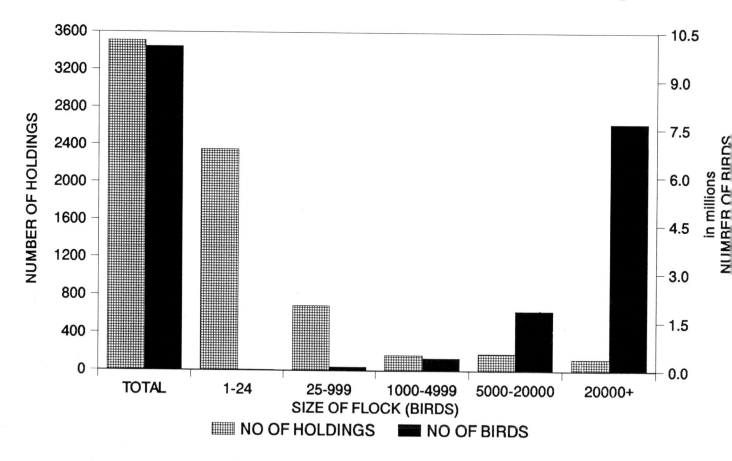

NUMBER OF LAYER FLOCKS AND BIRDS BY FLOCK SIZE: ENGLAND AND WALES

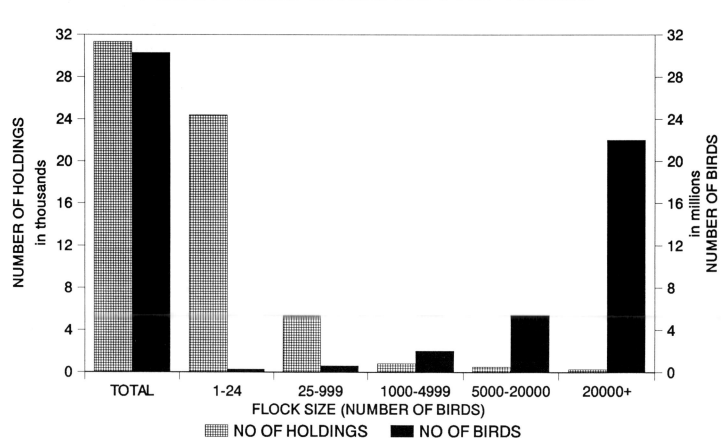

Summary of Conclusions and Recommendations

3.26 *Salmonella enteritidis* is well adapted to poultry and does not normally cause disease in adult birds. It does, however, have the ability to invade the bird and infect internal organs, and therefore the potential to infect an egg before it is laid.

3.27 The lower levels of human salmonella infection in Northern Ireland as compared with the rest of the UK, reported in Chapter 2, may be connected to the lower incidence of *Salmonella enteritidis* in its poultry flocks.

3.28 The incidence of *Salmonella enteritidis* in poultry has increased considerably between 1986 and 1989. No single cause for the rise has been identified from animal epidemiology, but it has been suggested that the infection was introduced via the elite stock and that the current strains of poultry stock are more susceptible to infection with *Salmonella enteritidis* phage type 4. There is currently very little evidence to support this. In addition, there is little evidence that feed now represents a major source of infection.

3.29 In common with other salmonella serotypes, *Salmonella enteritidis* is sometimes found in dust, litter and water within henhouses. Adequate cleaning and disinfection are needed to ensure that infection is not carried over to new stock. Difficulties may occur in cleaning a poorly designed henhouse, thus allowing salmonellae to remain in the henhouse environment to infect an incoming flock.

3.30 Small doses of organisms may lead to infection in poultry, and infection may be easily spread by aerosols. Vermin may also spread salmonella infection from one henhouse to another but their role in the epidemiology of the disease needs to be clarified. Poultry workers may also be a hazard, and it is therefore sensible for poultry workers to comply fully with measures designed to prevent cross-contamination from poultry workers to chickens and vice-versa.

3.31 Since the Government introduced its package of measures for the control of salmonella in poultry flocks in 1989, there has been a steady decline in the number of commercial egg laying birds that have been slaughtered. Infection is now being confirmed in fewer larger flocks and controls on breeding flocks are now fully operational. It is difficult to reconcile the high numbers of reports of *Salmonella enteritidis* in humans and the decline in the number of confirmed incidents in poultry flocks. We believe that Government can review its policy for the slaughter of commercial laying flocks.

CHAPTER 4

CONTAMINATION OF EGGS

How Eggs become Contaminated

4.1   Only recently has there been evidence to suggest that in-shell contamination of eggs with salmonella may occur and have significant consequences for public health. Before the increase in media attention on the association between the consumption of eggs and salmonellosis, and the issue of the Chief Medical Officer's advice, consumers had always considered eggs to be a safe food, and eggs have often been eaten raw or lightly cooked.

4.2   As explained in Chapter 3 (paragraph 3.2), it has been suggested that *Salmonella enteritidis* may invade the internal organs of poultry, and eggs may therefore be contaminated. We will look at the evidence for this in more detail in this Chapter. There are, however, several other routes by which eggs may be contaminated:

   i) direct faecal contamination of the shell; and

   ii) penetration of salmonella from the shell surface or environment into the egg contents.

4.3   In addition the contents of uninfected eggs can become contaminated once they have been broken out[g] if they come into contact with a contaminated egg or any contaminated food, persons or utensils. The possible importance of such cross-contamination in contributing to the current incidence of *Salmonella enteritidis* in humans will be considered in the next Chapter.

i) Faecal contamination of the shell

4.4   *Salmonella enteritidis* can be isolated from poultry faeces and can thus contaminate egg shells as a result of faecal contamination after lay. Faecal contaminants may find their way into eggs contents via cracks in the shell, when eggs are broken out, or if they are washed in water at temperatures which cause the contents to contract giving rise to negative pressure within the egg. If the storage temperature of the egg is allowed to fluctuate condensation may occur on the shell surface which may facilitate the passage of any salmonella present into the egg contents. When stored at ambient[h] temperature salmonellae may die out on shell surfaces after a few days, probably because of lack of moisture. We believe that more work should be done to ascertain exactly under what circumstances the organism might survive for longer periods of time.

ii) Penetration of salmonella from the shell surface

4.5   While it is not impossible that a single species such as *Salmonella enteritidis* could be particularly prone to pass through egg shells and associated membranes it is probable that other organisms are just as likely to contaminate the egg in a similar way, and one would expect to find these and other salmonellas as well in the contents, particularly as there is some evidence that *Salmonella enteritidis* competes badly with other organisms in the albumen of eggs stored at ambient temperature[32].

Ovarian or oviduct infection

4.6   Infection of the reproductive tissue is considered to be the major route by which egg contents

---

g   broken out eggs are those that have had their contents separated from their shells.

h   in the UK ambient temperature is generally accepted to be between 18°C and 22°C.

become infected. Infection of the ovary can give rise to infection in the yolk but is likely to give rise to deformed or defunct ovaries. In common with other salmonellas, *Salmonella enteritidis* can grow rapidly in yolk and has, when present in this site, been shown to survive a variety of forms of cooking[33].

4.7   Results from a series of studies using over 8,000 eggs have shown that 0.6% of the eggs from poultry flocks naturally infected with *Salmonella enteritidis* were positive for the organism and in the majority of these the level of contamination was low[34,35]. The storage of the eggs was shown to have no effect on the prevalence of salmonella positive eggs but did influence the levels of the organism in the contents. In eggs stored for up to 21 days all contained less than 20 bacteria per egg, but nearly half of those stored between 20°C and 21°C for more than 3 weeks contained more than 100 bacteria and of these two eggs had much higher levels of the organism. We believe that more work is required on the survival and levels of *Salmonella enteritidis* in eggs stored at a range of temperatures.

4.8   During the studies the egg shells were often tested in bulk. A number of different strains of salmonella were isolated from the shells but the contents yielded only *Salmonella enteritidis*. When the shells and contents of 1,952 eggs were identified and cultured separately, *Salmonella enteritidis* was isolated from the shells of 21 eggs and the contents of 18. Only one egg was positive on both sites. The site of contamination within the egg was identified for 15 salmonella positive eggs: *Salmonella enteritidis* was isolated from the albumen of 12, from the yolk of two, and from both sites in one egg.

4.9   These studies indicate that the principal site of contamination is probably the albumen. As there is no evidence to suggest that *Salmonella enteritidis* is more likely to penetrate the egg than other micro-organisms present on the shell surface it seems likely that eggs become infected in the course of their passage through the oviduct. Infection of the oviduct could arise as a result of systemic infection or retrograde infection from the cloaca. Further evidence to support this view of oviductal infection comes from studies on the eggs produced by hens infected artificially with *Salmonella enteritidis*[36,37,38].

4.10   In experiments designed to simulate "natural" contamination, eggs have been inoculated with approximately 10 cells of *Salmonella enteritidis*[38]. Under these conditions, growth in the albumen was governed by the age of the egg and proximity to the yolk. Significant growth did not take place when the eggs were less than 21 days old and if the organism was sited away from the yolk, (Appendix III, paragraph 20). Physical and chemical changes take place in the egg contents over time and the albumen and yolk membrane alters allowing nutrients or substances, particularly iron, to leak out of the yolk to support bacterial growth.

4.11   Some indication as to the relative importance of storage temperature comes from a small study undertaken to assess the growth of *Salmonella enteritidis* in eggs stored in the domestic environment. Eggs were inoculated close to the yolk with approximately 50 cells of *Salmonella enteritidis* at point of lay and stored at temperatures of either 20°C or where the temperature sometimes rose to 30°C. At 20°C no growth occurred during the first 21 days but under the simulated domestic conditions bacterial growth did occur in the albumen. These results provide some evidence to suggest that under certain storage conditions *Salmonella enteritidis* can grow in albumen during the initial three weeks after lay, and we therefore believe that it is particularly important that, as far as possible, eggs are stored under constant temperature regimes, which should not exceed 20°C.

The Extent of Contamination

4.12   Since 1990, the PHLS have examined samples of 60 eggs taken from consignments of imported eggs by Port Health Authorities. Samples from 1,068 and 863 consignments were examined in 1990 and 1991 respectively, representing 56% and 76% of all consignments imported in these years. Using the 1991 data, the PHLS estimated that for imported eggs the prevalence of contamination with all *Salmonella* species was 1:370 (95% confidence limits 1:440 - 1:320); the prevalence of contamination specifically with *Salmonella enteritidis* was 1:2,720 (95% confidence limits 1:4,270 - 1:1,740)[39].

4.13 In 1991, the PHLS also undertook a survey of salmonella contamination in British eggs sold through high street retail outlets. Salmonellae were isolated from 65 out of 7,045 boxes of 6 eggs: 47 boxes contained eggs contaminated with *Salmonella enteritidis* and 70% of these belonged to phage type 4. Thus *Salmonella enteritidis* was isolated from 0.7% of six-egg packs. In other words, 99.3% of the six-egg packs tested in the survey were found not to contain *Salmonella enteritidis* contaminated eggs. Overall the prevalence of contamination of British eggs with salmonella was estimated to be 1:650 (95% confidence limits 1:830 - 1:510), and for *Salmonella enteritidis* 1:880 (95% confidence limits 1:1,170 - 1:660)[40].

4.14 We understand that broadly similar results are emerging from a MAFF survey of British eggs collected from GB packing stations though this survey was primarily designed to compare salmonella contamination rates in home produced and imported eggs.

4.15 As part of its study of UK eggs, PHLS also looked at other factors that could affect the levels of Salmonella contamination. No difference was detected in the rate of contamination between free range and battery eggs with regard to any Salmonella species, but the presence of visible faecal matter was more frequently reported on contaminated eggs than uncontaminated ones. Faecal contamination of the shell and other routes by which eggs may become infected are discussed earlier in this Chapter.

4.16 The PHLS studies demonstrate that the overall level of contamination with salmonella is higher in imported than home produced eggs. However, the majority of salmonellas from imported eggs are not those frequently associated with human infection. In contrast, UK eggs are three times more likely to be contaminated with *Salmonella enteritidis* than imported eggs. The findings of the PHLS study, that 1:880 of British eggs are contaminated with *Salmonella enteritidis*, cannot be compared or contrasted with the findings reported in 4.7 since the latter relate only to contamination of the contents of eggs from flocks known to be infected with *Salmonella enteritidis*.

4.17 The PHLS studies have provided valuable information on the contamination of both UK and imported eggs and in the absence of any previous information they provide the baseline for future studies. We believe that further monitoring is needed to identify any trends in the prevalence of *Salmonella enteritidis* in UK or imported eggs. Similar studies should therefore be carried out and the results used as the basis for future comparison.

Summary of Conclusions and Recommendations

4.18 Eggs may become contaminated with *Salmonella enteritidis* if the organism comes into contact with the shell, but it is likely that infection of the reproductive tissue of the bird is the major route by which eggs become infected. Research suggests that 0.6% of eggs laid by an infected flock may be contaminated.

4.19 Where an egg is infected internally the albumen of the egg seems to be the principal site of contamination, although it appears that the age and temperature storage of an egg may have a direct bearing on the level of contamination within the albumen. Some studies have shown that the bacteriostatic properties of albumen function up to 21 days from lay, and any *Salmonella enteritidis* organisms present in the egg are likely to be there in small numbers only when eggs are held at temperatures not exceeding 20°C. After this time the bacteriostatic properties wane and the albumen cannot be relied upon to prevent bacterial multiplication. Low temperatures (below 8°C, see paragraph 2.1) must then be employed upon to control bacterial growth. In order to reduce the risk of salmonella infection from eggs we believe that eggs should be used while any bacteriostatic properties in the albumen are still effective, that is - with our current knowledge - within 3 weeks of lay. As far as possible, eggs should also be stored under constant temperature regimes, that do not exceed 20°C, to avoid condensation at the shell surface (paragraph 4.4). However only a small number of studies have been done in this area so far and more research is needed on the effects of storage on bacterial survival and the integrity of the albumen in relation to age.

4.20 The PHLS surveys on imported eggs and UK eggs at retail outlets indicate the approximate proportion of eggs that are contaminated with salmonella. Further studies to define this contamination more closely, and with narrower confidence limits, could be done only at disproportionate costs to the value of the results obtained. Nevertheless, we believe that similar studies to those of the PHLS, carried out at regular intervals, should suffice to monitor any important changes.

CHAPTER 5

EGG PRODUCTION, DISTRIBUTION AND PROCESSING

Production

5.1   In this Chapter we consider the laws and guidelines that dictate how eggs are produced, distributed and marketed in the UK.

5.2   We have been told that the number of UK poultry flocks in which *Salmonella enteritidis* infection has been confirmed is small set against the whole, and in addition, the PHLS surveys (paragraphs 4.12-4.17) have shown that 1 in 880 eggs produced in the UK are positive for salmonella at retail. The absolute number of eggs on sale that are contaminated with salmonella could therefore be large as in 1991 UK flocks produced 835 million dozen eggs[41] (ex-farm value £432 million) from 33 million laying hens[42].

5.3   Although eggs in 1991 were produced on 33,546 holdings, 69% of the egg output comes from 285 holdings which have flocks of 20,000 or more birds[42]. A schematic representation of the industry is presented at Appendix V Annex A.

5.4   Almost 90% of eggs for consumption are laid by hens kept in battery cages. Free range is estimated to represent some 5-7% of commercial sales nationally, but sales in the South East are higher at 10-15%, while in the North East of England the volume may still be less than 1% of sales. Figures from MAFF statistical surveys show battery production at 84%, free range at 10% and perchery at 6% with deep litter at insignificant levels (less than 1%).

5.5   The industry is split into two main groups. One consists of 5 companies which together produce 66% of the domestic production in Great Britain. These large companies either control all of their egg production and packing processes or sub-contract some parts on a strictly controlled basis. The other group comprises smaller producer packers and accounts for 34% of production of eggs.

Marketing

5.6   The marketing of eggs is controlled by the EC Egg Marketing Standards Regulations (Council Regulation 1907/90) and Commission Regulation 1274/91 (as amended by 3540/91 and 2221/92) which lay down common rules and standards relating to quality, weight, packaging, labelling, transport, presentation and marking/labelling of eggs and egg packs[43]. The information on egg marketing in the following paragraphs (5.7-5.14) is all in accordance with these Regulations.

5.7   The EC Regulations apply to all eggs marketed within the Community except eggs sold at the producer's own farm gate, on his own egg round or on his own stall at a local public market, provided the eggs are neither sold as graded by quality or weight nor packed in boxes which carry the information usually found on egg boxes.

5.8   Packing takes place on around 2,200 registered egg packing stations, many of which are on farm. Some 40 of these are major stations each handling the eggs from one or more large production farms. Only packing centres registered with the Ministry may grade and pack eggs. In order to be registered, packing centres must satisfy the conditions laid down in the Regulations and be inspected regularly by the Ministry's Egg Marketing Inspectorate. Scotland and Northern Ireland have their own Inspectorates.

5.9   Eggs have to be delivered to the packing stations at least every third working day, except where they can be stored on farm at ambient temperatures not exceeding 18°C, when delivery can occur once a week. These timescales are reduced where a laying date is to be indicated on the eggs at the packing station, or is marked on the egg on farm, and for eggs to be sold as Extra Fresh.

5.10 Packing centres grade and pack eggs at latest on the second working day following delivery; again there is a reduced timescale for eggs for which the laying date is to be indicated.

Labelling

5.11 There are mandatory markings for egg packs and various optional markings allowed both on egg packs and on Class A eggs themselves. Large and small egg packs must show the name and address of the packer or retailer who has had the eggs packed, the centre name and number, the quality and weight gradings, the number of eggs packed and the packing date. The information which may be stamped on eggs includes quality and weight grades, packing centre name and/or number, a reference to the type of farming under which the eggs were produced, and an origin mark.

5.12 In addition to the packing date, a sell by date and/or best before date may also be indicated at the time of packing on the egg boxes and/or the eggs. The laying date may also be stamped on the eggs either at the packing station or, subject to certain conditions, at the farm. In addition, detailed records are required to be kept by both the producer (who must be registered with MAFF) and the packer; and the production unit and the packing centre must be inspected at least every two months. Where a recommended sell-by date is indicated this must be the latest date that eggs should be offered for sale to the consumer, after which there remains a reasonable storage period of at least seven days in the home when the egg retains Grade A characteristics; the best before date is the last day of this storage period.

5.13 We believe that the EC Regulations allow for confusion over the labelling of eggs because both sell-by and best before labels can be used. Marking eggs with either of these dates is not in the best interest of the consumer who would benefit more from a simple use-by date.

Storage and Retailing

5.14 There is a general requirement in the Directive that eggs shall be maintained, both during storage at the producer's premises and during transport from the producer to the collection or packing centre, at a temperature best suited to ensure optimal conservation of their quality. Bacterial multiplication will be substantially reduced or prevented if eggs are adequately refrigerated, and ideally, eggs would be refrigerated throughout the transport and retail chain. However, the refrigeration of Grade A eggs on retail premises or elsewhere in the marketing chain below +5°C is prohibited by the Directive to ensure that quality standards are maintained. There is a limited derogation for eggs which have been kept at a temperature below +5°C during transport of not more than 24 hours or on retail premises, provided the quantity stored does not exceed the requirements for 3 days of retail sale. We believe that more work is needed on the effect of refrigeration on the preservation of egg quality.

5.15 As shell eggs are not listed as a "relevant food" in the Food Hygiene (Amendment) Regulation 1990[44] or 1991[45] there is no requirement for eggs to be stored at anything other than ambient temperatures at retail.

5.16 As explained in paragraphs 4.10 and 4.11, the albumen maintains bacteriostatic properties for a period of time after lay. In general, eggs are likely to be distributed and marketed during this time and we therefore urge the industry to regard eggs as short shelf-life products and recommend a use by date of 3 weeks. Eggs may be kept safely during this period if storage, distribution and retail temperatures do not exceed 20°C and they are maintained at a constant temperature to avoid any problem from condensation. Small retail outlets especially will need to take account of this, particularly in warm weather, and they should make arrangements to see that any eggs for sale are stored at temperatures not exceeding 20°C.

5.17 After purchase, however, we suggest that it would be prudent for consumers and caterers to store eggs in a refrigerator as cooking procedures carried out in the kitchen are likely to cause temperatures fluctuations in the environment and on occasion may rise considerably above 20°C.

Storing eggs in the refrigerator at a temperature below 8°C will also reduce any bacterial growth that might occur after the bacteriostatic properties of the albumen wane.

5.18 It is estimated that about 90% of eggs produced for human consumption are sold ''in shell'' (around 757 million dozen per annum). The remainder (about 78 million dozen eggs) are processed to produce bulk liquid, frozen or dried whole egg, yolk or albumen or for use in the production of other foods (Appendix V).

Pasteurisation of Eggs

5.19 Pasteurised egg is used as an ingredient in a wide range of foods produced both for retail and for the catering market, which may in turn require further processing or incorporation into other products prior to sale. There are approximately 20 egg pasteurisation plants in the UK which produce chilled, dried or frozen pasteurised egg.

5.20 Rules governing the egg pasteurisation process are laid down in the EC Egg Products Directive 89/437[46] which came into force on 31 December 1991. This Directive requires absence of salmonella in the finished product. Eggs from UK flocks infected with *Salmonella enteritidis* may now be processed by pasteurisation, although we understand that this is not current industrial practice.

Summary of Conclusions and Recommendations

5.21 Although the number of UK poultry flocks in which *Salmonella enteritidis* is confirmed at any one time is small, and only a small percentage of the eggs laid by an infected flock are believed to be contaminated, the total number of infected eggs marketed will be large as the UK produces some 835 million dozen hen's eggs per year for human consumption.

5.22 EC Regulations lay down both mandatory and optional markings for eggs and egg packs. Both can be marked with a sell-by or best before date, but the pack must be marked with a packing date. Although packing dates and sell-by dates are both of use to the producer and retailer, we believe that only a use-by date on the pack is of help to the consumer, and eggs should therefore be marked with this date.

5.23 Multiplication of any salmonella present in eggs will be substantially reduced if eggs are adequately refrigerated, ie below 8°C. There is no legal requirement for eggs to be stored at other than ambient temperature at retail, and as the time from lay to sale is likely to be short, and this will be within the the period that the albumen maintains its bacteriostatic properties, we believe that they can be stored in retail premises at, but not exceeding, 20°C providing they are stored in constant temperatures to avoid any problems from condensation. However, in order to ensure that eggs are stored below 20°C after purchase, eggs should be stored in a refrigerator. Storing eggs at below 8°C in this manner will also ensure that any bacterial growth after the bacteriostatic properties wane. Further studies need to be undertaken on the effect of refrigeration on the preservation of egg quality.

CHAPTER 6

USE AND HANDLING OF EGGS

6.1   In addition to being a nutritious food, eggs are a common item in the UK diet. With proper handling and adequate cooking this valuable commodity should provide safe foods free from salmonella and other food pathogens. In this Chapter we look at how eggs are handled and used both in catering and in the domestic environment, and consider the importance of cross-contamination of eggs and foods containing eggs in relation to the current incidence of human salmonellosis.

Eggs in Catering

Traditional Catering Practice

6.2   Caterers frequently use eggs as ingredients or as the main element of a meal. Some of the traditional recipes used in catering operations include the use of raw egg (whole and separate) which will not be cooked prior to consumption. For example, mayonnaise (which appears to be the commonest vehicle in most of the reported outbreaks), mousses, royal icing and marzipan may include raw egg as an ingredient, further examples are in Appendix VI. Other recipes and dishes, for example, fried, poached or boiled eggs, omelettes and scrambled eggs may receive only light cooking where the temperatures reached may be low and not sufficient to destroy pathogens like salmonella. Adequate cooking is particularly difficult when the egg is placed on a cold or frozen centre for example, baked alaska or meringue toppings.

Use of Pasteurised Eggs in Catering

6.3   Until 1989 caterers made little use of pasteurised egg. The product was only supplied in containers above 5 kilogrammes and more often in half ton tanks, but today pasteurised egg is supplied to the caterer in containers ranging from 1 to 10 litres.

6.4   Some parts of the catering industry still use shell eggs as raw ingredients for some products but we have been told that the larger catering companies have moved towards using pasteurised egg as an ingredient for mousses, scrambled egg, omelettes etc. Food manufacturers and bakers use pasteurised egg almost exclusively for baking as either an ingredient or a glaze.

6.5   Since 1989 caterers have also been purchasing more factory manufactured mayonnaise which invariably uses pasteurised egg. Another change seen in some sectors of the catering industry has been the change to the use of convenience foods containing eggs such as mousses.

6.6   Some dried products also contain pasteurised egg, for example powders which on reconstitution are used by bakers and caterers to make custards or vanilla slices etc. The powders may be reconstituted by the addition of cold water and are used where microbiological quality is critical to the safety of the end product.

6.7   A more recent innovation is frozen egg nuggets which are individually quick frozen (IQF) granules made from pasteurised whole egg. These are used to make scrambled egg, or for incorporation into other products prepared by the caterer. Cooked scrambled egg in chilled or frozen form can also be supplied by some companies specialising in foods containing eggs.

6.8   There are three reasons why the catering industry is increasingly using pasteurised rather than shell egg:-

> i) caterers are heeding advice from the Chief Medical Officer on the dangers of eating raw eggs and uncooked dishes made from them[1,2];

ii) caterers have become aware of the safety issues surrounding the use of raw shell eggs and are gradually moving towards using what is considered to be a much safer product; and

iii) in some catering operations breaking out eggs can be a time-consuming operation and it may be more cost-effective for the caterer to purchase pasteurised egg, rather than pay staff to do a laborious task.

Storage of Eggs in Catering

6.9   There appears to have been some confusion amongst caterers about the storage of shell eggs. There is currently no requirement for eggs to be kept refrigerated at retail (see paragraph 5.15), and historically the caterers' perception of egg has been that of a safe product. Although many caterers are aware of the dangers of handling raw meats, especially poultry, few apparently regard shell eggs as requiring the same level of caution. Liquid pasteurised egg and foods containing eggs should always be kept refrigerated.

Future Developments

6.10   The catering industry has many small businesses, and therefore there is great difficulty in getting relevant advice disseminated. Environmental Health Officers probably have the greatest influence on the food hygiene standards within small catering operations, particularly where the manager or proprietor is not a member of a professional body and thus does not receive guidance from such sources.

6.11   The Government Code of Practice No. 9 on Food Hygiene Inspections advises that Environmental Health Officers pay particular attention to the control of hazards in the premises which they are inspecting[47]. The principles of hazard analysis critical control point systems (HACCP) used in some sectors of the manufacturing industry are being promoted by central Government to Environmental Health Departments and to all sectors of the food and catering industries. The assessment of the potential hazards in catering operations and their prevention could include an analysis of the hazards presented by the use of eggs and foods containing eggs.

6.12   The 1990 and 1991 amendments to the Food Hygiene (General) Regulations and the greater emphasis on temperature control may have some effect on the way in which foods containing eggs are made and stored in catering outlets[44,45]. In any case, foods containing eggs should be kept refrigerated to help reduce multiplication of any salmonellae present.

6.13   The use of shell egg, pasteurised egg and other egg products in catering operations are now more likely to come under scrutiny as changes in the legislation have made many organisations more aware of their catering practices, and of the need for training, good hygiene and the serving of safe food to customers. The Food Safety Act 1990[48] gives the Government powers to require the training of food handlers, and national Regulations will be introduced requiring training for some food handlers.

Eggs in the Domestic Kitchen

6.14   In contrast to the situation in the catering industry, most of the eggs eaten in the home are shell eggs rather than pasteurised eggs. Eggs are a common item in the domestic kitchen, and are often eaten boiled, poached or fried. Eggs also form the major component of a number of recipes either home-made or purchased as ready or partially prepared dishes (Appendix VI).

6.15   There is little published research on the hygiene practices or cooking arrangements in domestic kitchens, although we are aware that some work is being funded by Government in this area at Strathclyde University. We believe that more studies should be done to get a clearer picture of the way in which eggs are handled in the home.

6.16 Salmonellae can survive for a period of time on the shells of eggs (paragraph 4.4), on equipment, work surfaces and on the hands. More needs to be known about the factors that influence the length of time that the organisms survive in these environments so that better advice can be given to consumers and caterers.

6.17 Traditional teaching and recipe books published before 1989 provide methods for producing food that include the use of raw and partially cooked shell eggs, but some recently published cookery books have taken account of the advice of the Chief Medical Officer[1,2] and do not include recipes for uncooked egg dishes made with raw egg.

6.18 There are a number of dishes cooked very lightly or not at all that are considered ''classical'' dishes and which require raw egg or some part of them which cannot be substituted or removed, for example meringue and mousse which require raw albumen. These dishes are not prepared everyday in the domestic kitchen, and are more likely to be made as a treat or for a special occasion.

6.19 Most of the traditional and classical dishes can now be purchased from supermarkets either chilled or frozen and ready prepared, and the market in these convenience foods has increased in recent years. It should be noted that the eggs used in manufactured products are mostly pasteurised, but that some small specialist retail outlets still use shell eggs to make foods such as cheesecakes and quiches.

6.20 Pasteurised, frozen or dried egg replacements can be found in some retail shops, although they are not always readily available, and may not be sold in suitably sized packs. Consumers seem not to regard these products highly and some consumers are simply unaware of their existence. We believe that more effort by retailers should be made to bring the benefits of using pasteurised eggs to the attention of their customers.

Storage of Eggs in the Home

6.21 The Government advises people to store eggs in a refrigerator when issuing public information on food safety. Not surprisingly, however, we have been informed that a number of consumers do not understand why eggs that are purchased at ambient temperature should be stored differently in the home. More should be done to explain to consumers why eggs should be kept cool.

Importance of Cross-Contamination

6.22 It is the practice in some catering operations to break out eggs prior to a peak demand period so that the egg is readily on hand when the customer requires a meal. In particular, broken-out eggs may be whisked in a bowl and left adjacent to the cooking range so that omelettes can be made on demand.

6.23 When the contents of an egg are broken out any organisms present in the albumen will have access to nutrients from the yolk and multiplication will be possible. Clearly, one egg which contains a number of organisms when added to others will provide an inoculum for the larger volume. Similarly, the eggs could become contaminated from a separate source. If they are then left at ambient temperature and used to make foods which are not cooked, there is an opportunity for the organism to multiply. Because of this, broken-out eggs need to be handled carefully, and if they are not to be used immediately for cooking they must be stored covered in a refrigerator, and only for a limited period of time. Once containers are opened, pasteurised egg should be treated in the same way as broken-out shell egg. Liquid pasteurised egg should always be stored under refrigeration.

6.24 Cross-contamination during the storage and the general preparation of food is believed to play an important part in many outbreaks, which may also involve eggs or foods containing egg, contaminated from another source. It is an accepted problem, the scale of which is difficult to judge. However, we do not believe that the observed increase in salmonella incidence can be explained by cross-contamination alone.

Summary of Conclusions and Recommendations

6.25 The egg within its shell is different in many ways from raw liquid egg. Once eggs are broken out and held at ambient temperature they provide a good medium for bacterial multiplication. Great care must be taken with this commodity; if it is not for immediate cooking it must be stored covered in the refrigerator. Raw eggs should not be used in uncooked foods, and when eggs are required for these dishes pasteurised eggs should be used.

6.26 Caterers are making more use of pasteurised egg, although it seems that domestic consumers are not. The risk of illness could be reduced if consumers substituted pasteurised egg for shell egg when producing foods where the egg content is either not cooked or not cooked to a sufficiently high temperature to destroy salmonella.

6.27 Consumers have not been well informed of the reasons why eggs should be refrigerated after purchase and may therefore be continuing to store them at ambient temperatures in the home. We believe that they should be encouraged to store eggs in the refrigerator.

Cross-contamination

6.28 Cross-contamination plays a role in human salmonella infection but it is difficult to make any kind of assessment of the part it plays as there has been little research carried out in this area. It may be that raw poultry and eggs with contaminated shells are the main sources from which cross-contamination with salmonella occurs in the kitchen.

CHAPTER 7

CONCLUSIONS

Epidemiology

<u>Salmonella in Humans</u>

7.1   From 1981 to 1991 there has been a rise of over 170% in the reported number of cases of salmonella in humans, primarily because of an increase in *Salmonella enteritidis* infections, particularly *Salmonella enteritidis* phage type 4.

7.2   Other countries in the world, notably in Europe and the USA, have seen similar rises in human salmonellosis which appears to have started at about the same time as that in the UK.

7.3   Northern Ireland has a lower rate of human salmonellosis than the rest of the UK. Human isolations there have steadily declined since 1987, and it is possible that this decrease is connected to the successful control of *Salmonella enteritidis* in their poultry flocks.

7.4   Most cases of salmonella infection occur sporadically. Salmonella outbreaks contribute only a small proportion of cases to the total number of reported illnesses. Salmonella surveillance data shows that the number of general outbreaks in the UK has not significantly increased in recent years, despite the increase in cases.

7.5   Although it is not clear why *Salmonella enteritidis* has become the predominant serotype causing human infection in the UK rather than any other serotype, it is most probable that it is due to its presence in certain foods, in particular eggs and poultry.

7.6   Microbiological and epidemiological data from the UK and abroad have shown a strong association between *Salmonella enteritidis* and the consumption of eggs and poultry or foods containing them. Data from thoroughly investigated salmonella outbreaks, while not always providing direct evidence to identify the source(s) of infection, have provided strong indirect evidence that eggs have been the source in *Salmonella enteritidis* phage type 4 outbreaks. In many investigations the putative vehicle of infection is no longer available for testing and is not traceable back to the supplier. Therefore, there is currently insufficient information available to enable us to assess what proportion of cases are due to the consumption of eggs and foods containing eggs.

<u>Salmonella in Poultry</u>

7.7   *Salmonella enteritidis* is well adapted to poultry and does not normally cause disease in adult birds. It does, however, have the ability to invade the bird and infect internal organs, and therefore the potential to infect an egg before it is laid.

7.8   The incidence of *Salmonella enteritidis* in poultry has increased considerably since 1986, but it is now being found in a decreasing number of large flocks. No single cause for the rise has been identified from animal epidemiology, but it has been suggested that the infection was introduced via the elite stock and that the current strains of poultrystock are more susceptible to infection with *Salmonella enteritidis* phage type 4. There is currently very little evidence to support this. In addition, there is little evidence that feed now represents a major source of infection.

7.9   In common with other salmonella serotypes, *Salmonella enteritidis* is sometimes found in dust, litter and water within henhouses. Adequate cleaning and disinfection are needed to ensure that infection is not carried over to new stock. Difficulties may occur in cleaning a poorly designed henhouse, thus allowing salmonellae to remain in the henhouse environment to infect an incoming flock.

7.10 Small doses of organisms may lead to infection in poultry, and infection may be easily spread by aerosols. Vermin may also spread salmonella infection from one henhouse to another but their role in the epidemiology of the disease needs to be clarified. In addition, the possibility of infection being transmitted on the clothes and footwear of personnel should not be overlooked, and poultry workers should adopt specific measures to prevent cross-contamination from poultry workers to poultry flocks and vice-versa.

Government Control Measures on Salmonella in Poultry

7.11 Since the Government introduced its package of measures for the control of salmonella in poultry flocks in 1989, there has been a steady decline in the number of commercial egg laying birds that have been slaughtered. Infection is now being confirmed in fewer large flocks, and controls on breeding flocks are fully operational. It is difficult to reconcile the high numbers of reports of *Salmonella enteritidis* in humans and the decline in the number of confirmed incidents in poultry flocks, and we therefore believe that Government could review its policy for the slaughter of commercial laying flocks.

Contamination of Eggs

7.12 Eggs may become contaminated with *Salmonella enteritidis* if the organism comes into contact with the shell, but it is likely that infection of the reproductive tissues of the bird is the major route by which eggs become infected. Research suggests that 0.6% of eggs laid by an infected flock may be contaminated.

7.13 Where an egg is infected internally the albumen of the egg seems to be the principal site of contamination, although it appears that the age and temperature storage of an egg may have a direct bearing on the level of contamination within the albumen. Some studies have shown that the bacteriostatic properties of albumen function up to 21 days from lay and any *Salmonella enteritidis* organisms present in the egg are likely to be there in small numbers only, when eggs are held at temperatures not exceeding 20°C. After this time the bacteriostatic properties wane and the albumen cannot be relied upon to prevent bacterial multiplication. Low temperatures (below 8°C, see paragraph 2.1) must then be employed upon to control bacterial growth. In order to reduce the risk of salmonella infection from eggs we believe that eggs should be used while any bacteriostatic properties in the albumen are still effective, that is - with our current knowledge - within 3 weeks of lay. As far as possible, eggs should also be stored under constant temperature regimes, that do not exceed 20°C, to avoid condensation at the shell surface (paragraph 4.4). However, only a small number of studies have been done in this area so far and more research is needed on the effects of storage on bacterial survival and the integrity of the albumen in relation to age.

7.14 The PHLS surveys on imported eggs and eggs at retail outlets indicate the approximate proportion of eggs that are contaminated with salmonella. Further studies to define more closely levels with narrow confidence limits could be done only at disproportionate cost to the value of the results obtained. Nevertheless we believe that similar studies to those of the PHLS, carried out at regular intervals, should suffice to monitor any important changes.

Egg Production, Marketing and Processing

7.15 Multiplication of any salmonella present in eggs will be substantially reduced if eggs are adequately refrigerated, ie below 8°C. There is no legal requirement for eggs to be stored at other than ambient temperature at retail, and as the time from lay to sale is likely to be short, and this will be within the the period that the albumen maintains its bacteriostatic properties, we believe that they can be stored in retail premises at, but not exceeding, 20°C providing they are stored in constant temperatures to avoid any problems from condensation. However, in order to ensure that eggs are stored below

20°C after purchase, eggs should be stored in a refrigerator. Storing eggs at below 8°C in this manner will also restrict any bacterial growth after the bacteriostatic properties wane. Further studies need to be undertaken on the effect of refrigeration on the preservation of egg quality.

7.16   Although the number of UK poultry flocks in which *Salmonella enteritidis* is confirmed at any one time is small, and though only a small percentage of the eggs laid by an infected flock are believed to be contaminated, the total number of infected eggs marketed will be large as the UK produces some 835 million dozen hen's eggs per year for human consumption.

7.17   EC Regulations lay down both mandatory and optional markings for eggs and egg packs. Both can be marked with a sell-by or best before date, but the pack must be marked with a packing date. Although packing dates and sell-by dates are both of use to the producer and retailer, we believe that only a use-by date is of help to the consumer, and eggs should therefore be marked with this date.

Use and Handling of Eggs in Catering and the Domestic Kitchen

7.18   The egg within its shell is different in many ways from raw liquid egg. Once eggs are broken out and held at ambient temperature they provide a good medium for bacterial multiplication. Great care must be taken with this commodity; if it is not for immediate cooking it must be stored covered in the refrigerator. Raw eggs should not be used in uncooked foods, and when eggs are required for these dishes pasteurised eggs should be used.

7.19   Caterers are making more use of pasteurised egg, although it seems that domestic consumers are not. The risk of illness could be reduced if consumers substituted pasteurised egg for shell egg when producing foods where the egg content is either not cooked or not cooked to a sufficiently high temperature to destroy salmonella, and we believe that they should be encouraged to do so.

7.20   Consumers have not been well informed of the reasons why eggs should be refrigerated after purchase and may therefore be continuing to store them at ambient temperatures in the home. We believe that they should be encouraged to store eggs in the refrigerator.

Cross-Contamination

7.21   Cross-contamination plays a role in human salmonella infection but it is difficult to make any kind of assessment of the part it plays as there has been little research carried out in this area. It may be that raw poultry and eggs with contaminated shells are the main sources from which cross-contamination with salmonella occurs in the kitchen.

CHAPTER 8

RECOMMENDATIONS

Advice to Consumers

8.1 We **endorse** the advice given by the Chief Medical Officer in 1988 that: "people should avoid eating raw eggs or uncooked foods made from them and that vulnerable people such as the elderly, the sick, babies and pregnant women should consume only eggs which have been cooked until the white and yolk are solid".

Handling and Storage of Eggs

8.2 We have noted that the EC Regulations on egg marketing encourage a maximum temperature of 18°C for eggs on farms (paragraph 5.9). To maintain the bacteriostatic properties of the albumen and to avoid problems of condensation, during the storage, distribution and retail chain, we believe that eggs should as far as possible, be maintained at a constant temperature that does not exceed 20°C (see paragraph 8.6) and should not be subjected to large fluctuations in storage temperature. In addition we believe that eggs should be marketed and used as soon as possible after lay. **We therefore recommend that eggs should be consumed within 3 weeks from date of lay**.

8.3 In order to implement our recommendation in paragraph 8.2 above, changes will be needed to the way in which eggs are labelled when they are sold. We have noted that the labelling of eggs is not consistent with other EC food labelling legislation. At present the only mandatory date marking on egg packs is the date of packing (paragraph 5.11). The EC Regulations on marketing standards for eggs states that additional date marks can be stamped on the egg packs and/or on the eggs themselves. Many packing centres already label egg packs with either a sell-by or a best-before date which is of some help to the consumer provided that the eggs are stored in the pack, but a use-by date would be of more use to the consumer. **We recommend that eggs should be labelled with a use-by date and that retailers should encourage the industry to mark egg packs with this date, and extend the date marking to the eggs themselves**. This labelling should pay due regard to our recommendation that eggs should be consumed within 3 weeks of lay.

8.4 In addition, we believe that all users of shell eggs should be encouraged to treat eggs as a short shelf-life product. Storing eggs in a refrigerator below 8°C will help maintain a constant storage temperature as well as maintaining "quality". This 8°C will also reduce the growth of any *Salmonella enteritidis* that might be present in the egg (parapragh 2.1) if the bacteriostatic properties of the albumen start to wane. **We therefore recommend that, once purchased, eggs should be stored in the refrigerator, below 8°C, both in the home and in catering premises. We further recommend that the labelling of eggs should include storage information.**

8.5 There appears to be some confusion amongst caterers and consumers as to the correct way to store eggs (paragraphs 6.9 and 6.21). **We recommend that the Government should seek to increase public awareness of the correct way to store eggs both in the home and in catering premises**.

8.6 The EC Regulations on marketing standards for eggs includes certain aspects of handling and storage of eggs on farm, at the packing centre, in store and during transport (paragraphs 5.6-5.10 and 5.14). We believe that eggs should be stored and transported within a system, not exceeding 20°C, which avoids excessive temperature fluctuations. **We recommend that the industry, together with the retailers, should draw up a Code of Practice for the handling and storage of eggs during the egg production chain from point of lay to retail**. This Code, which should take account of the EC Regulations, would be of benefit to all those involved in the production and marketing of eggs.

Use of Pasteurised Egg

8.7   The risk of human infection from raw or partially cooked eggs will be considerably reduced if pasteurised egg rather than shell egg is used whenever possible. In catering we find the increased use of pasteurised egg as opposed to shell egg in the catering industry encouraging (paragraphs 6.3-6.8), and **recommend that caterers should continue to increase their use of pasteurised egg, particularly for dishes that are not subject to further cooking prior to consumption**.

8.8   Domestic consumers should consider making more use of pasteurised egg. Although pasteurised egg is available, it has been suggested to us that consumers either do not regard it as an alternative to shell egg or are simply unaware that it exists (paragraph 6.20). **We recommend that manufacturers and retailers, together with consumer organisations, should consider how best to encourage consumers to use pasteurised egg instead of shell egg, where appropriate.**

Training of Food Handlers

8.9   National Regulations requiring training of some food handlers will be introduced (paragraph 6.13). We were pleased to hear that the industry has taken steps to improve food safety training in anticipation of the Regulations, and **we support the introduction of mandatory training of food handlers and recommend that food hygiene training programmes should pay particular attention to the correct handling of eggs and foods containing eggs and the avoidance of cross contamination**.

Improvements in the Monitoring/Reporting of Outbreaks of Foodborne Illness

8.10   The quality of the data collected from investigations of salmonella outbreaks is variable. We believe that more guidance should be given to all those with a responsibility in this area on how such investigations should be carried out (paragraph 2.24) and **we therefore recommend that the Departments of Health in the UK should consider ways of improving the quality of investigations of outbreaks and their documentation**.

8.11   We were pleased to see that, in accordance with a recommendation of the ''Richmond'' Committee on the Microbiological Safety of Food, the DEP (Division of Enteric Pathogens) and CDSC (Communicable Disease Surveillance Centre) databases which maintain information on the incidence of human salmonella infections have been amalgamated (paragraph 2.4). We believe that the new reporting system is a considerable improvement over the old system, and **we recommend that the new CDSC reporting forms should be used to report investigations as fully as possible**.

8.12   The majority of cases of human salmonellosis are apparently sporadic and because of practical difficulties are seldom investigated. Outbreaks are more amenable to investigation and clues about the vehicles of infection are more easily obtained. While it may be that vehicles responsible for outbreaks are the same as those responsible for sporadic cases, this may not always be so. The Human Epidemiology Working Group of the Steering Group on the Microbiological Safety of Food is currently assessing the feasibility of undertaking national studies on the incidence of foodborne disease in the community (paragraph 2.14). **We recommend that the Steering Group on the Microbiological Safety of Food: Human Epidemiology Working Group should identify suitable mechanisms by which epidemiological investigations of sporadic cases could be undertaken to improve identification of sources and vehicles of infection and consider whether such studies could be undertaken cost-effectively.**

Government Measures for the Control of Salmonella in Poultry

8.13   We have been encouraged to see that since Government controls were introduced in 1989 the number of large laying flocks in which *Salmonella enteritidis* has been confirmed has declined. Since these flocks produce some 70% of the UK's home produced eggs, and controls on breeding flocks are now fully operational and *Salmonella enteritidis* is rarely found in feedstuffs, we believe that the Government's policy for the compulsory slaughter of commercial laying flocks infected with this organism should be reviewed. **We therefore recommend that the Government review the continuing need for the compulsory slaughter of laying flocks infected with** *Salmonella enteritidis.*

8.14 We believe that the recommendation from the "Richmond" Committee on the Microbiological Safety of Food on guidelines on the hygienic design of broilerhouses, should now be extended to the design of henhouses (paragraph 3.7), but that the guidelines should be prepared by industry in close consultation with the Government. **We recommend that these guidelines should cover the design, construction and maintenance of buildings for breeding and egg laying flocks, with particular regard to effective cleansing and disinfection between flocks and minimising introduction of infection to birds**.

8.15 It is important that the risk of salmonella getting into a flock once the birds have been introduced into the poultryhouse is minimised. **We recommend that MAFF, in consultation with the industry, should consider updating the 1988 MAFF/British Poultry Federation Code of Practice on the Control of Salmonellae in Commercial Laying Flocks and the 1988 Code of Practice for Poultry Health Scheme Members on the Control of Salmonellae** (paragraph 3.8).

8.16 In order to progress recommendations 8.13 to 8.15 above, **we recommend that a liaison team should be set up by Government to monitor the progress of the industry towards the goal of reducing the incidence of salmonella in poultry**. The work of the team will be primarily for industry with the Government acting as a catalyst.

Research and Surveillance

8.17 In order to improve the current understanding of the sources of *Salmonella enteritidis* and possible routes of infection for human disease, **we recommend that Government should commission further research in the following areas** :-

i) **sub-typing of** *Salmonella enteritidis* for epidemiological purposes (paragraph 2.28);

ii) the **survival of** *Salmonella enteritidis* and other *Salmonella* species **on the hands; shells of intact eggs; equipment** and **work surfaces** (paragraphs 4.4 and 6.16);

iii) **effects of storing eggs at ambient and refrigeration temperatures on the survival of** *Salmonella enteritidis* (paragraphs 4.7 and 7.13); and

iv) **the integrity of albumen in relation to age and the effect of refrigeration on the preservation of egg quality** (paragraph 7.15).

8.18 In addition **we recommend that more work should be done on kitchen practice in the domestic and catering environment** (paragraph 6.15) **and that Government should seek to use the results of such work to target its public information on good hygiene practice.**

8.19 **We recommend that the Government should undertake more research to determine whether competitive exclusion could have a useful role to play in minimising the risk of** *Salmonella enteritidis* **infection in laying flocks** (paragraph 3.9).

Surveillance Studies

8.20 **We recommend that Government should consider funding regular surveys on the incidence of** *Salmonella enteritidis* **in imported eggs and UK eggs on retail sale** (paragraph 4.15).

APPENDIX I

LIST OF RESPONDENTS

The Committee would like to thank the following organisations and individuals who contributed written information:-

University of Bristol - School of Veterinary Science;

Central Veterinary Laboratory, Ministry of Agriculture Fisheries and Food;

Communicable Disease (Scotland) Unit;

Co-op Wholesale Society Ltd;

Department of Agriculture for Northern Ireland;

Department of Health;

DLO Spelderholt Centre for Poultry Research and Information Services (Netherlands);

Professor J P Duguid;

Food and Drink Federation;

Leatherhead Food Research Association;

National Farmers Union;

Nigel Horrox Veterinary Group;

Ministry of Agriculture Fisheries and Food;

Public Health Laboratory Service;

Salmonella Task Force - United States Department for Agriculture;

J Sainsbury plc.

APPENDIX II

ACKNOWLEDGEMENTS

The Advisory Committee would like to express their grateful thanks to Mr R Ackerman (Hotel and Catering Training Company), Professor R Board (University of Bath), Mr D Clarke (Trusthouse Forte), Mr P Day (Agricultural Development Advisory Service), Mr H Hellig (British Veterinary Association), Dr M Hinton (University of Bristol), Dr T J Humphrey (Public Health Laboratory Service), Dr R M McCracken (Department of Agriculture for Northern Ireland), Dr G Mead (University of Bristol), Mr R North (Independent Food Safety Advisor), Dr B Rowe (PHLS), Dr C Wray (Central Veterinary Laboratory, Ministry of Agriculture, Fisheries and Food) and Messrs Howie, Beckett, Leal, Kemp and Ring (British Egg Industry Council) for the written and oral evidence that they submitted to the Working Group. A summary of the major points made by these witnesses is included at Appendix III.

APPENDIX III

SUMMARY OF THE MAIN POINTS MADE TO THE WORKING GROUP BY THE EXPERTS WHO GAVE ORAL EVIDENCE

Human Epidemiology

1.   Human infection with *Salmonella enteritidis* has increased in the last five years.

2.   *Salmonella enteritidis* is found within food i.e. in egg contents and poultry meat muscle. Foods infected in this way are more of a risk to human health than those infected on the surface only.

3   Infection may occur in a healthy person after eating a single egg if the number of viable organisms in it constitute a large enough dose.

4.   There is a need for improved investigation of foodborne outbreaks and more accurate reporting of vehicles and sources of infection.

Animal Epidemiology

5.   At the same time that a rise in the incidence of *Salmonella enteritidis* was detected in the UK, rises in the occurrence of this organism were also detected in other countries. However, such occurrences were not always of the same strain or even phage type.

6.   *Salmonella enteritidis* may have become more invasive in recent years than in the 1970s, but this is not necessarily due to a change in the virulence of the organism.

7.   No specific reason can be identified for the observed increase of *Salmonella enteritidis* in poultry since 1986, although a number of suggestions have been put forward. For example, it may have started as a point source outbreak in the elite breeder stock. The initial vehicle of infection may have been feed, including raw materials and additives, or infection could have come from a contaminated vaccine or probiotic.

8.   The microbiological quality of feed has been improved with the implementation of a comprehensive system of testing feed ingredients. Large layer and broiler breeders companies manufacture and control the quality of their own feed. There is no evidence to suggest that feed had represented a major source of salmonella infection, although it remains a possibility.

9.   Recent structural changes within the poultry industry have led to more intensive production facilities with higher stocking densities and increased turnover of stock. This might provide greater opportunity for the spread of infection.

Genetics

10   The number of strains used as the source of broiler and laying hens is very limited and under the control of a few companies in Europe.

11.   Genetics may have a role in determining the susceptibility of a particular strain to infection, but there is little current data to indicate that this is so.

Environment

12.   *Salmonella enteritidis* can survive in the soil and can therefore be found in buildings on poultry farms.

13.   Small doses of organisms can lead to the infection of birds.

14.   Infection in poultry may easily be spread by aerosols, and this is especially true for birds managed on the floor system.

15.   Although vermin and other forms of wildlife may spread infection from one hen house to another they probably do not cause the initial contamination. It is more likely that they are an indication of infection in the environment.

16.   Better cleaning techniques need to be employed in henhouses and improvements are needed in the design of cleaning equipment, so that it can do the job adequately, especially in battery laying sheds.

17.   Workers in the poultry industry who are infected with salmonella may transmit the disease to flocks while handling the birds.

Eggs

18.   Internal infection of eggs probably occurs mostly as they pass through the oviduct, where the albumen is infected. The oviduct may become infected via the blood-stream or in a retrograde way from the cloaca.

19.   Research has shown that 0.6% of eggs laid by an infected flock are infected internally. In an infected flock 3% of the eggs laid by an individual hen may be contaminated and there is clustering with a number of hens laying contaminated eggs at or around the same time.

20.   The age of the egg and refrigerated storage have a direct bearing on the number of organisms which may be present within the egg. At 21 days and over there may be a multiplication of *Salmonella enteritidis* inside eggs held at ambient temperature. The albumen becomes less bacteriostatic as it ages, and nutrients also pass from the yolk to the albumen which allow the organisms to grow. Refrigeration can help prevent this increase.

Catering

21.   Changes in food preparation processes may provide greater opportunity for cross-contamination in food.

22.   More meals are now produced by caterers which might have led to an increase in the number of incidents of *Salmonella enteritidis.*

23.   There has been an increase in the use of poultry and mayonnaise which is likely to have increased the risk of infection to consumers from these foods.

24.   Sales of pasteurised foods containing eggs have increased as a result of caterers making a conscious decision to switch from shell eggs.

25.   Date marking of bulk packed eggs supplied to caterers do not give any indication of the shelf life, and some are supplied without any labelling at all.

26.   The need for training in the hotel and catering industry is recognised, and most of the larger organisations provide training in house. Small companies may find it difficult to provide the necessary training.

Northern Ireland

27.   Northern Ireland have, up to now, been successful in maintaining an uninfected national flock.

28.   The small size of the industry has resulted in easier containment and control of *Salmonella enteritidis* when the problem was recognised.

29.   In addition, they have strict quarantine for imported breeding stock, have encouraged heat-

treatment of feed for many years, and have cleanable concrete floors for all henhouses.

Government Slaughter Policy

30.   The present monitoring and slaughter policy for poultry has had some effect but difficulties have occurred due to the *Salmonella enteritidis* present in the environment. It is generally considered to be effective in the control of infection in the breeding birds, but some experts consider it inappropriate for commercial layers because of the degree of environmental contamination on-farm.

31.   The antibody status of birds cannot be relied upon to indicate their state of infection. In order to satisfy the criteria in the Zoonoses Order 1989 for testing and slaughter, the organism has to be isolated from faeces and internal organs.

Factors which could help to Improve the Situation

32.   More needs to be known about the virulence of the organism, whether this has changed in recent years, the colonisation of the chicken gut, and possible resistance factors in chickens.

33.   Plasmid profiling would be a helpful epidemiological tool to help trace the spread of infection.

34.   Continued microbiological monitoring at hatcheries followed by appropriate action to resolve the problem when infection occurs will ensure that breeding stock is free of infection.

35.   To help prevent the continued infection of poultry stock there is a need for uncontaminated feed and henhouses designed hygienically to enable thorough cleaning.

36.   Competitive exclusion and vaccines may also be able to play a part in prevention of infection in the future.

37.   More attention should be given to human carriers of salmonella infection working in the poultry industry.

38.   Under controlled conditions egg could be washed effectively and without risk to their microbiological status.

39.   The shelf-life of eggs should be required to be no longer than 10 days from packing.

40.   A simple Use by date would give caterers a better indication of storage life.

41.   Caterers and consumers need to store eggs in the refrigerator to extend their microbiological quality beyond 21 days.

42.   Better training would help improve hygiene awareness in commercial and consumer kitchens, but developing mechanisms of information transfer to small businesses remains a challenge.

APPENDIX IV

TABULATED DATA ON EPIDEMIOLOGY

SALMONELLA IN HUMANS

ENGLAND AND WALES

YEAR	S typhimurium		S. enteritidis				Other Serotypes		Total
			PT4		Other PT's				
1981	3992	(39)	392	(4)	695	(7)	5172	(50)	10251
1982	6089	(49)	413	(3)	688	(6)	5132	(42)	12322
1983	7785	(51)	823	(5)	951	(7)	5596	(37)	15155
1984	7264	(49)	1362	(9)	709	(5)	5392	(37)	14727
1985	5478	(41)	1771	(13)	1324	(10)	4765	(36)	13330
1986	7094	(42)	2979	(17)	1792	(11)	5111	(30)	16976
1987	7660	(37)	4962	(24)	1896	(9)	6014	(30)	20532
1988	6444	(23)	12522	(46)	2905	(11)	5607	(20)	27478
1989	7306	(24)	12931	(43)	2842	(10)	6919	(23)	29998
1990	5451	(18)	16151	(54)	2689	(9)	5821	(19)	30112
1991	5331	(19)	14693	(53)	2767	(10)	4902	(18)	27693

SOURCE - DEP DATA ( ) =%

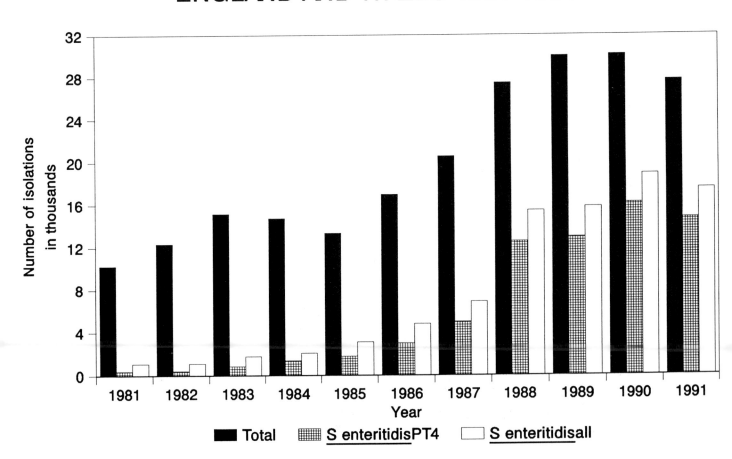

SALMONELLA IN HUMANS
ENGLAND AND WALES 1981-1991

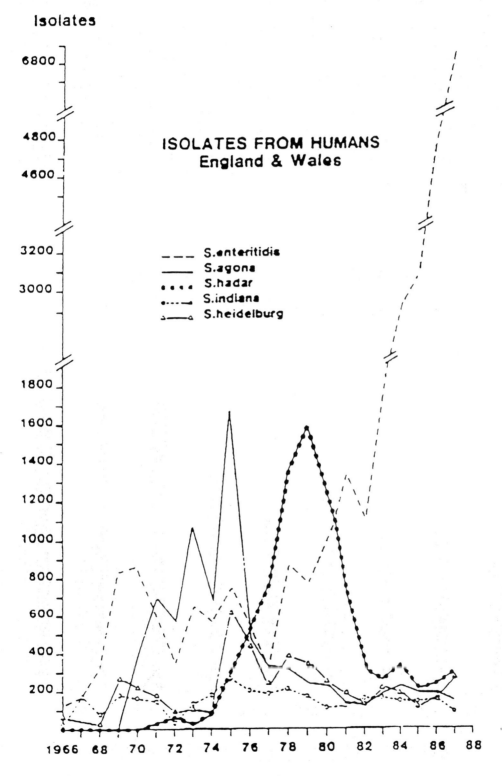

Isolates

ISOLATES FROM HUMANS
England & Wales

_ _ _ _ S.enteritidis
———— S.agona
• • • • S.hadar
•—··—• S.indiana
▵———▵ S.heidelburg

Source.Strains referred to Division of Enteric Pathogens

SALMONELLA IN HUMANS

NORTHERN IRELAND

YEAR	S typhimurium		S enteritidis*				Other Serotypes		Total
			PT4		Other PT's				
1981	43	(33)			8	(6)	80	(61)	131
1982	38	(34)			1	(1)	74	(65)	113
1983	49	(35)			12	(9)	80	(57)	141
1984	31	(24)			8	(6)	91	(70)	130
1985	36	(31)			8	(7)	71	(62)	115
1986	106	(45)			59	(25)	70	(30)	235
1987	133	(31)	162	(37)	63	(14)	77	(17)	435
1988	43	(21)	78	(37)	36	(17)	49	(24)	205
1989	36	(17)	27	(13)	36	(17)	108	(52)	207
1990	32	(12)	75	(29)	103	(39)	51	(20)	261
1991	34	(21)	31	(19)	16	(10)	79	(49)	160

( ) =%

* Prior to 1987 information on PT not available

SALMONELLA IN HUMANS
NORTHERN IRELAND 1981-1991

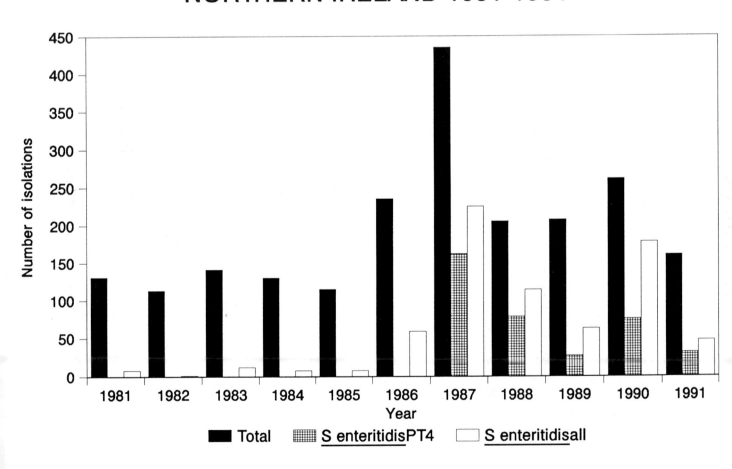

SALMONELLA IN HUMANS

SCOTLAND

YEAR	S typhimurium		S enteritidis PT4		Other PT's		Other Serotypes		Total
1980	522	(33)	28	(2)	85	(5)	842	(60)	1577
1981	1117	(44)	37	(1)	213	(8)	1159	(45)	2526
1982	1286	(49)	42	(2)	237	(9)	1076	(41)	2621
1983	1201	(52)	80	(3)	239	(10)	768	(34)	2288
1984	1069	(48)	183	(8)	250	(11)	719	(32)	2221
1985	689	(41)	138	(8)	380	(23)	473	(28)	1690
1986	646	(32)	282	(14)	336	(17)	750	(37)	2015
1987	679	(30)	587	(26)	381	(15)	669	(29)	2286
1988	733	(28)	910	(35)	435	(17)	507	(20)	2580
1989	532	(21)	1116	(43)	286	(11)	644	(25)	2578
1990	606	(25)	1078	(44)	163	(7)	594	(24)	2441
1991	505	(22)	1102	(47)	163	(7)	474	(24)	2338

SALMONELLA IN HUMANS
SCOTLAND 1980-1991

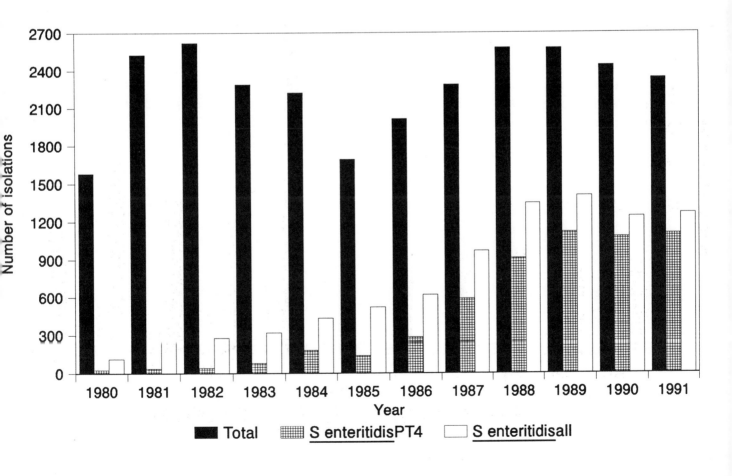

APPENDIX V - NOTES

STRUCTURE OF POULTRY AND EGG INDUSTRY

Structure of the Poultry and Egg Industries

1.   Although related, the poultrymeat and egg sectors are essentially separate businesses with stock being bred for either eating or laying purposes.

2.   In both industries there are three categories of stock:

i) <u>Elite (Great Grandparent)</u> - Are in-bred family groups carrying certain genetic qualities. Most of this stock is produced outside the UK.

ii) <u>Grandparent</u> - Are bred from the best of the elite lines to carry the particular characteristics required. Parent stock are produced from these birds. Foreign breeders usually maintain flocks in the UK at Grandparent level.

iii) <u>Parent</u> - Are used to produce fertile eggs for either broiler or layer breeders. They are situated on multiplying farms many of which are in the hands of independent producers on contract to hatcheries.

Poultry Industry

3.   For broiler strains of parent stock there are only two companies of significance involved in breeding in the UK, one is UK based and the other in the US.

4.   The egg industry plays an important role in UK agriculture and eggs represent about 4% of the total output of agricultural commodities.

5.   UK egg production is carried out on 33,546 holdings with 33 million laying hens producing 835 million dozen eggs per year with a value of £432 millions ex-farm. The industry is split into two main groups, the first consists of 5 companies who together account for 66% of production. These companies are run on integrated lines and either control all processes or on a strictly controlled basis sub-contract some parts. The other group consist of small producer packers and account for 34% of production.

Schematic representation of the Poultry and Egg Industry

Elite (grandparent)
Mostly produced outside the UK. Bred for genetic characteristics

↓

Grandparent
Foreign breeders maintain flocks in the UK at this level. Use best elite stocks for appropriate birds.

↓

Parent
Produce broilers or layers at multiplication farms. Usually in the hands of independent producers on contract to hatcheries. Two main strains of layers in the UK, both produce brown eggs. ISA of French origin and the Eurobird Hi-sex Brown of Dutch origin. Also two main strains of broilers, Cobb and Ross

650 million broiler chicks per annum

↓

Broilerhouses

↓

Slaughter

Hatchery
Produce day old chicks

Rearing House
Rear chicks to 18 week - point of lay

↓

Laying houses
33, 546 holdings
33 million hens
(Census figures)

Battery
About 90% of production

Free Range
About 5-7% of production nationally. (Uneven distribution, 10-15% in the South East and less than 1% in the North East).

Perchery
About 4% of production

Deep Litter
Small numbers

↓

835 million dozen eggs per annum (Source: AUK) £432 million ex farm.

↓

Packing Stations
2200 stations, 40 major ones. Many packing stations are on farm

10% of eggs   90% of eggs

Processing
Liquid, frozen, dried, whole egg, yolk or albumen, bakery products etc. About 78 milion dozen per annum

Shell eggs
For human consumption, about 757 million dozen eggs per annum

Export
8132 tonnes per annum.
16 milion dozen eggs

Industry
Incorporation into other products

Retail

Import
21,216 tonnes per annum.
57 million dozen eggs

RECIPES CONTAINING EGGS

The following is a list of food dishes which contain eggs classified according to the amount of cooking received by the eggs.

Raw Eggs

Almond paste
Andalouse sauce
Aspic (egg white whipped in for glaze)
Bavarois
Butter icing
Bombe (homemade)
Caesar salad
Cassata ice cream
Charlotte Russe
Coleslaw
Crevettes Marie Rose
Egg flip
Egg mayonnaise
Eggnog

Fluffs
Gateau St Honore
Gnocchi
Green Sauce
Ice cream (home made)
Marie Rose sauces
Marzipan
Mayonnaise
Mousses
Parisienne Gnocchi
Peppermint creams
Piedmontaise Gnocchi
Potato salad
Remoulade
Romaine Gnocchi

Salmon mayonnaise
Sandwiches (binding)
Shellfish cocktail
Souffles incl.
Milanaise
Sorbets Stuffed eggs
Steak Tartare
Tartare sauce
Tyrolienne sauce
Vegetable salad
Verte sauce
Waldorf salad
Water ices
Zitti (homemade)

Lightly cooked Egg

Apple meringue
Flan/Banana flan
Baked Alaska
Bavarois
Bearnaise
Blanquette de Veau
Brioch potatoes (glaze)
Boiled egg*
Buck Rarebit
Charlotte Russe
Chicken a la King
Chicken Veloute
Choron
Coconut Filling
Consomme Royale (garnish)
Duchesse potatoes (glaze)

Egg custard sauce
En cocotte
Fricasse de Volaille
Fried egg (hot or cold)*
Gateau St Honore
Ground Rice
Hollandaise sauce
Lemon meringue pie
Marshmallows
Marquise potatoes (glazed)
Meringues
Mille-feuille
Omelette
Oeufs a la Neige
Pastry cream
Pavlova
Poached egg
Queen of Puddings
Quiches

Rice pudding
Sabayon
Sago
Sandwich filling
Savoury flans
Scrambled eggs
Scotch Woodcock
Semolina
Shepherd's Pie (glaze)
Souffle incl.
Milanaise
Sur le plat (egg)
Tapioca
Thermidor
Welsh Rarebit
White Chaud-froid sauce
White wine sauce (garnish)
Zabaglione

Medium Cooked Eggs

Baked egg custard
Boiled egg*
Bread and butter pudding

Cabinet pudding
Creme caramel
Croquettes (coating)

Fried egg (hot or cold)*
Pouding Souffle
Souffles
Savoury flans

Well Cooked Eggs

Baked egg custard
Boiled eggs*

Croquettes

Fried egg*

*amount of cooking depends on personal taste.
Compiled by Dr Susan C Morgan-Jones, Scottish Office Agriculture and Fisheries Department and Mrs Barbara McInally, Department of Catering, Fashion and Design, Ayr College.

APPENDIX VII

CHARACTERISTICS OF GRADE A EGGS
as laid down in the EC Regulation No 1274/91

1. Grade ''A'' eggs shall have the following minimum characteristics :-

    Shell and cuticle : normal, clean, undamaged;

    Air space : height not exceeding 6 mm; stationary; however, for eggs to be marked as ''extra'', it shall not exceed 4 mm at the time of packing or time of customs clearance in the case of imports;

    White : clear, limpid, of gelatinous consistency, free of extraneous matter of any kind;

    Yolk : visible on candling as a shadow only, without clearly discernible outline, not moving appreciably away from the centre of the egg on rotation, free of extraneous matter of any kind;

    Germ cell : imperceptible development;

    Odour : free of extraneous odour.

2. Grade ''A'' eggs shall not be washed or cleaned by any other means before or after grading.

3. Grade ''A'' eggs shall not be treated for preservation or refrigerated in premises or plants where the temperature is artificially maintained at less than +5°C. However, eggs which have been kept at a temperature below +5°C during transport of not more than 24 hours or on retail premises or in the annexes thereto, shall not be considered as refrigerated in so far as the quantity stored in these annexes does not exceed the requirements for three days of retail sale on the premises in question.

REFERENCES

1. Department of Health: Salmonella and Raw Eggs. London: Department of Health, 1988 (Press Release 88/285).

2. Department of Health: Salmonella and Eggs. London: Department of Health, 1988 (Press Release 88/409).

3. House of Commons Select Committee on Agriculture. Salmonella in Eggs. London: HMSO, 1989.

4. House of Commons Select Committee on Agriculture. Salmonella in Eggs - A Progress Report. London: HMSO, 1989.

5. The Committee on the Microbiological Safety of Food. The Microbiological Safety of Food: Part II: Report of the Committee on the Microbiological Safety of Food to the Secretary of State for Health, the Minister of Agriculture, Fisheries and Food and the Secretaries of State for Wales, Scotland and Northern Ireland. London: HMSO, 1991.

6. Baird-Parker A C Foodborne Salmonellosis. Lancet review of foodborne illness. Edward Arnold 1991. Chapter 8 pages 53-61.

7. The Committee on the Microbiological Safety of Food. The Microbiological Safety of Food: Part I: Report of the Richmond Committee on the Microbiological Safety of Food to the Secretary of State for Health, the Minister of Agriculture, Fisheries and Food and the Secretaries of State for Wales, Scotland and Northern Ireland. London: HMSO, 1990.

8. HMSO - The Zoonoses Order 1989. Statutory Instrument 1989 No. 285. HMSO 1989.

9. Rodrigue D C, Tauxe R V and Rowe B - International Increase in *Salmonella enteritidis*: A New Pandemic? Epidemiology and Infection 1990; 105: 21-27.

10. WHO Surveillance Programme for Control of Foodborne Infections and Intoxications in Europe. Fifth Report, 1985-1989. Berlin: WHO, 1992.

11. St.Louis M.E, Morse D.L, Potter E.M, De Melfi T.M, Guzewich J.J, Tauxe R.V. and Blake P.A. - The Emergence of grade A eggs as a major source of *Salmonella enteritidis* infections. New implications for the control of salmonellosis. Journal of the American Medical Association, 1988; 259, 2103-2107.

12. Perez J, Tello O, Mata M. and Fuente E.- Foodborne infections and intoxications - outbreaks evolution in Spain : 1976-1984. Proceedings of 2nd World Congress on Foodborne Infections and Intoxications, 1984 Berlin.

13. Perales I, Audicana A - *Salmonella enteritidis* and eggs. Lancet 1988; ii 1133.

14. Perales I, Audicana A - The role of hens' eggs in outbreaks of salmonellosis in north Spain. International Journal of Food Microbiology 1989; 8: 175-180.

15. Fantasia M, Filetici E, Anastasio M P et al - Italian experiance in *Salmonella enteritidis* 1978-1988: Characterisation of isolates from food and man. International Journal of Food Microbiology 1991; 12: 353-362.

16. Anon. Veterinary Public Health. Salmonella control by immunisation of animal. WHO Weekly Epidemiological Record 1990; 65: 243.

17. PHLS unpublished provisional data.

18. Palmer S R - Epidemiological methods in the investigation of outbreaks of foodborne disease. Proceedings of the Third World Congress of Foodborne Infections and Intoxications. 1992; Berlin.

19. Coyle E.F, Palmer S.R., Ribeiro C. D - *Salmonella enteritidis* phage type 4 infection: association with hens' eggs. The Lancet, 1988; ii: 1295-1297.

20. Cowden J.M, Lynch D, Joseph C.A, O'Mahoney M, Mawer S.L, Rowe B. and Bartlett C.L.R. - Case-control study of infections with *Salmonella enteritidis* phage type 4 in England. British Medical Journal, 1989; 299: 771-773.

21. Ministry of Agriculture, Fisheries and Food, Welsh Office Agriculture Department and Department of Agriculture and Fisheries for Scotland - Animal Salmonellosis 1991 (in press).

22. The Expert Group on Animal Feedingstuffs - The Report of the Expert Group on Animal Feedingstuffs, chaired by Professor Eric Lamming, to The Minister for Agriculture, Fisheries and Food, The Secretary of State for Health and the Secretaries of State for Wales, Scotland and Northern Ireland.

23. Ministry of Agriculture, Fisheries and Food and the British Poultry Federation - Code of Practice for the Control of Salmonellae in Commercial Laying Flocks (1988).

24. Ministry of Agriculture, Fisheries and Food - Code of Practice for Poultry Health Scheme Members for the Control of Salmonellae (1988).

25. Mead G.C. - Developments in competitive exclusion to control salmonella carriage in chickens. Proceedings of the International symposium on colonisation control of human bacterial enteropathogens in poultry, Atlanta. 1991. **To be published**.

26. Ministry of Agriculture, Fisheries and Food:
Code of Practice for the Control of Salmonellae in the production of final feed for livestock in premises producing over 10,000 tonnes per annum (1989); and
Code of Practice for the Control of Salmonellae in the production of final feed for livestock in premises producing less than 10,000 tonnes per annum (1989).

27. Ministry of Agriculture, Fisheries and Food - Code of Practice for the Control of Salmonellae during the storage, handling and transport of raw materials intended for incorporation into animal feedingstuffs (1989).

28. Ministry of Agriculture, Fisheries and Food - Code of Practice for the Control of Salmonellae in Broilers (1989).

29. <u>HMSO</u> - Animal Health Act 1991.

30. <u>HMSO</u> - The Poultry Laying Flocks (Testing and Registration etc) Order 1989. Statutory Instrument 1989 No.1964, HMSO 1989.

31. <u>HMSO</u> - The Poultry Breeding Flocks and Hatcheries (registration and testing) Order 1989. Statutory Instrument 1989 No.1963.

32. <u>Dolman J & Board R.G.</u> - The influence of temperature on the behaviour of mixed bacterial contamination of the shell membrane of the hen's egg. Epidemiology and Infection, 1992. 108(1); 115-121.

33. <u>Humphrey T.J, Greenwood M, Gilbert R.J, Rowe B and Chapman P.A.</u> - The survival of salmonellas in shell eggs cooked under simulated domestic conditions. Epidemiology and Infection, 1989. 103: 35-45.

34. <u>Humphrey T.J, Baskerville A, Mawer S, Rowe B & Hopper S.</u> - *Salmonella enteritidis* phage type 4 from the contents of intact eggs. A study involving naturally infected hens. Epidemiology and Infection 1989. 103: 415-423.

35. <u>Humphrey T.J, Whitehead A, Gawler A.H.L, Henley A & Rowe R.</u> - Numbers of *Salmonella enteritidis* in the contents of naturally contaminated hens eggs. Epidemiology and Infection, 1991. 106: 489-496.

36. <u>Humphrey T.J, Baskerville A, Chart H, Whitehead A.</u> - Infection of laying hens with *Salmonella enteritidis* phage type 4 by conjunctival challenge. **To be published in the Veterinary Record**.

37. <u>Baskerville A, Humphrey T.J, Fitzegeorge R.B, Cook R W, Chart H, Rowe B & Whitehead A.</u> - Airborne infection of laying hens with *Salmonella enteritidis* phage type 4. Veterinary Record, 1992. 130(18); 395-398.

38. <u>Clay C.E.and Board R.G.</u> - Growth of *Salmonella enteritidis* in artificially contaminated hens' shell eggs. Epidemiology and Infection, 1991. 106: 271-281.

39. PHLS Unpublished provisional data.

40. PHLS Unpublished provisional data.

41. Ministry of Agriculture, Fisheries and Food - Agriculture in the UK: 1991, HMSO 1992.

42. Ministry of Agriculture, Fisheries and Food - Agricultural Census Data, (press releases 218/91 and 19/92)

43.   - <u>European Commission</u> Regulation Number 1907/90 of 26 June 1990 on certain marketing standards for eggs (OJ L173 of 6 July 1990) (see also Corrigendum in OJ L195 of 26 July 1990)

     - <u>European Commission</u> Regulation 1274/91 of 15 May 1991 introducing detailed rules for implementing Regulation 1907/90 on certain marketing standards for eggs (OJ L121 of 16 May 1991) (see also Corrigendum in OJ L233 of 22 August 1991)

     - <u>European Commission</u> Regulation 3540/91 of 5 December 1991 amending Regulation 1274/91 introducing detailed rules for implementing Regulation 1907/90 on certain marketing standards for eggs (OJ L335 of 6 December 1991)

     - <u>European Commission</u> Regulation 2221/92 of 31 July 1992 amending Regulation 1274/91 introducing detailed rules for implementing Regulation 1907/90 on certain marketing standards for eggs (OJ L218 of 1 August 1992)

44. <u>HMSO</u> The Food Hygiene (Amendment) Regulations 1990. Statutory Instrument 1990 No. 1431 Food. HMSO 1990.

45. <u>HMSO</u> The Food Hygiene (Amendment) Regulations 1991. Statutory Instrument 1990 No. 1343 Food. HMSO 1991.

46. <u>European Council</u> Directive No. 89/437 of 20 June 1989 on hygiene and health problems affecting the production and placing on the market of egg products (OJ L212 of 22 July 1989).

47. <u>HMSO</u> - Food Safety Act 1990 - Code of Practice No 9: Food Hygiene Inspections, London: HMSO 1991. 48. <u>HMSO</u> - The Food Safety Act 1990, Chapter 16. HMSO London 1990.

BIBLIOGRAPHY

Agriculture Review in the United Kingdom - MAFF
Response of government to the first report on salmonella in eggs - 1988/89 session.
Progress Report - Report and proceedings of committee & minutes of evidence and appendices (1990).
Response of government to progress report on salmonella in eggs - 1989/90 session.

Baker R.C. - Survival of *Salmonella enteritidis* on and in shelled eggs, liquid eggs, and cooked foods containing eggs. Dairy, Food and Environmental Sanitation, 1990. 10(5): 273-275.

Bleem A. - Layer industry blamed, but helpless in controlling S enteritidis. Feedingstuffs October 14 1991. 18-20. de Boer E & Hahne M. - Cross-contamination with Campylobacter jejuni and Salmonella spp. from raw chicken products during food preparation. Journal of Food Production, 1990. 53(12): 1067-1068.

Bolder N.M, van Lith L.A.J.T & Mulder R.W.A.W. - Production of *Salmonella enteritidis* contaminated eggs after inoculation of laying hens. Proceedings of the 10th symposium on the quality of poultry meat; safety and marketing aspects, ed. Mulder & de Vries, Doorwerth, The Netherlands, 12-17 May 1991.

Bolder N.M & van Lith L.A.J.T. - Production of *Salmonella enteritidis* PT4-three day old chickens. Proceedings of the 10th symposium on the quality of poultry meat; safety and marketing aspects, ed. Mulder & de Vries, Doorwerth, The Netherlands, 12-17 May 1991.

Bryant E.S. - *Salmonella enteritidis* control. Dairy, Food and Environmental Sanitation, 1990. 10(5): 271-272.

Bumstead N. & Barrow P.A. - Genetics of resistance to Salmonella typhmurium in newly hatched chicks. British Poultry Science, 1988. 29: 521-529.

Cooper G.L, Nicholas R.A. & Bracewell C.D - Serological and bacteriological investigations of chickens from flocks naturally infected with *Salmonella enteritidis*. Veterinary Record, 2 December 1989. 567-572.

Cowden J.M, O'Mahoney M, Bartlett C.L.R, Rana B, Smyth B, Lynch D, Tillett H, Ward L, Roberts D, Gilbert R.J, Baird-Parker A.C. and Kibsbey D.C. - A national outbreak of S typhimurium DT 124 caused by contaminated salami sticks. Epidemiology and Infection, 1989. 103: 219-225.

Cowden J.M, Chisholm D, O'Mahoney M, Lynch D, Mawer S.L, Spain G.E, Ward L. and Rowe B. - Two outbreaks of S enteritidis PT4 infection associated with the consumption of fresh shell-foods containing eggs. Epidemiology and Infection, 1989. 103: 47-52.

Curnow J. - *Salmonella enteritidis* associated with Duck Egg Consumption. Communicable Disease and Environmental Health Scotland Weekly Report, 1992. 26(7): 4-5.

Duguid J.P. & North R.A.E. - Eggs and salmonella food poisoning: an evaluation. Journal of Medical Microbiology, 1991. 34: 65-72.

Gast R.K. & Beard C.W. - Current ARS research on *Salmonella enteritidis* in chickens: experimental infections in laying hens. Dairy, Food and Environmental Sanitation, 1990. 10(5): 276-278.

Gill O.N, Sockett P.N, Bartlett C.L.R, Vaile M.S.B, Rowe B, Gilbert R.J, Dulake C, Murrell H.C. & Salmaso S. - Outbreak of S napoli caused by contaminated chocolate bars. Lancet, 12 March 1983. 574-577.

Hasenson L.B, Kaftyreva L, Laszlo V.G, Woitenkova E & Nesterova M. - Epidemiological and Microbiological data on *Salmonella enteritidis*. Acta Microbiologica Hungarica, 1992. 39(1): 31-39.

Healing T.D. - Salmonella in rodents: a risk to man? Communicable Disease Report 1991. 1(10): 114-116.

Hubert B, Dehaumont P & Pignault A. - Incidence of food poisoning in France 1989. Bulletin Epidemiologique Hebdomadaire, 1990. 16: 65-67.

Humphrey T.J, Baskerville A, Chart H & Whitehead A. - *Salmonella enteritidis* PT4 infection in SPF hens: influence of infecting dose. Veterinary Record, 1991. 129: 482-485.

Humphrey T.J, Cruickshank J.G & Rowe B.- Investigation of meeting of 6 outbreaks of egg associated *Salmonella enteritidis*. The Lancet, 4 February 1989.

Humphrey T.J. - Growth of salmonellas in intact shell eggs. Influence of storage temperature. Veterinary Record, 24 March 1990. 292.

Humphrey T.J, Chapman P.A, Rowe B and Gilbert R.J - A comparative study of the heat resistance of salmonellas in homogenized whole egg, egg yolk or albumen. Epidemiology and Infection, 1990. 104: 237-241.

Humphrey T.J, Baskerville A, Chart H & Rowe B. - Infection of egg laying hens with *Salmonella enteritidis* PT4 by oral inoculation. Veterinary Record, 18 November 1989. 331-332.

Lee J.A. - Recent trends in human salmonellosis in England and Wales: the epidemiology of prevalent serotypes other than *Salmonella typhimurium*. J. Hyg. Camb., 1974. 72: 185-195.

Lock J.L & Board R.G. - Persistence of contamination of hens' egg albumen in vitro with salmonella serotypes. Epidemiology and Infection, 1992. 108: 389-396.

Madden J.M. - *Salmonella enteritidis* Contamination of whole chicken eggs. Dairy, Food and Environmental Sanitation, 1990. 10(5): 268-270.

O'Mahoney M, Cowden J, Smyth B, Lynch D, Hall M, Rowe B, Teare E.L, Tettman R.E, Rampling A.M, Cole M, Gilbert R.J, Kingcott E, Bartlett C.L.R. - An outbreak of S saint-paul infection associated with beansprouts. Epidemiology and Infection, 1990. 104: 229-235.

Mandal B.K & Brennand J. - Bacteriamias in salmonellosis: a 15 year retrospective study from a regional infectious diseases unit. British Medical Journal Volume, 12 November 1988. 297.

Mitchell E, O'Mahony M, Lynch D, Ward L.R, Rowe B, Utley A, Rogers T, Cunningham D.G and Watson R. - Large outbreak of food poisoning caused by S typhimurium definitive type 49 in mayonnaise. British Medical Journal, 14 January 1989. 298: 99-101.

Morris G.K. - *Salmonella enteritidis* and eggs: assessment of risk. Dairy, Food and Environmental Sanitation, 1990. 10(5): 279-281.

North R.A.E - Letter to the editor of Environmental Health News, 30 August 1991.

Palmer S.R. - The investigation of food poisoning. Letters in Applied Microbiology, 1991. 12: 145-148.

Palmer S.R & Swan A.V. - The Epidemiological approach to infection control. Reviews in Medical Microbiology, 1991. 2: 187-193.

Pether J.V.S and Gilbert R.J. - The survival of salmonellas on finger tips and transfer of the organisms to foods. J. Hyg. Camb., 1971. 69: 673-681.

PHLS/SVS - Update on Salmonella Infection: Editions 1-13, October 1989 - October 1992.

Radford S.A, Tassou C.C, Nychas G.J.E, & Board R.G. - The influence of different oils on the death rate of *Salmonella enteritidis* in homemade mayonnaise. Letters in Applied Microbiology, 1991. 12: 125-128.

Roberts D. - Salmonella in chilled and frozen chicken. The Lancet, April 20 1991. 984.

Rowe B, Begg N.T, Hutchinson D.N, Dawkins H.C, Gilbert R.J, Jacob M, Hales B.H. and Rae F.A. - *Salmonella ealing* infections associated with the consumption of infant dried milk. The Lancet, 17 October 1987. 900-903.

Salmon R.L, Palmer S.R. Ribriro et al - How is the source of food poisoning outbreaks established? The example of three consecutive *Salmonella enteritidis* PT4 outbreaks linked to eggs. Journal of Epidemiology and Community Health, 1991. 45(4): 266-269.

Sekers S. - Killing with kindness. Sunday Telegraph, 20 October 1991.

Sesma B, Alvarez M.J, Aramendia P, Goni B, de Pablo N and Goni P - Extra-intestinal isolation of salmonella in hens : An epidemiological study of two outbreaks of salmonellosis caused by consumption of raw egg Microbiologia Seminar, 1987. 3: 209-212.

Schroeter A, Pietzscho O, Steinbeck A et al - Epidemiologische Untersuchungen zum *Salmonella enteritidis* - Geschenen in der Bundesrepublik Deutschland 1990. Bunndesundheitblatt 1991. 34:(4): 147-151.

Stevens A, Joseph C, Bruce J, Fenton D, O'Mahony M, Cunningham D, O'Connor B and Rowe B. - A large outbreak of S enteritidis PT4 associated with eggs from overseas. Epidemiology and Infection, 1989. 103: 425-433.

Thorns C.J, Sojka M.G, and Chasey D. - Detection of a novel fimbrial structure on the surface of *Salmonella enteritidis* by using monoclonal antibody. Journal of Clinical Microbiology, November 1990. 2049-2414.

WHO Surveillance programme for the control of foodborne infections and intoxications in Europe. Newsletter No. 31, February 1992.

WHO Veterinary Public Health - Salmonella control by immunisation of animals. Epidemiological Record, 3 August 1990. 31: 243.

Printed in the United Kingdom for HMSO

Dd 0294591 C22 1/93